A Retreat With Mary of Magdala and Augustine

# Other titles in the
## A Retreat With... *Series:*

# A RETREAT WITH
# MARY OF MAGDALA AND AUGUSTINE

## Rejoicing in Human Sexuality

## Sidney Callahan

## ST. ANTHONY MESSENGER PRESS

Cincinnati, Ohio

Scripture citations are taken from the *New Revised Standard Version Bible*, copyright ©1989 by the Division of Christian Education of the National Council of Churches of Christ in the U.S.A. and used by permission.

The excerpt from *Jesus, the Liberator of Desire*, copyright ©1989 by Sebastian Moore, is reprinted by permission of the author.

Excerpts from *Mating* by Norman Rush, copyright ©1991 by Norman Rush. Reprinted by permission of Alfred A. Knopf, Inc.

Cover illustrations by Steve Erspamer, S.M.
Cover and book design by Mary Alfieri
Electronic format and pagination by Sandra Digman

ISBN 0-86716-262-7

Published by St. Anthony Messenger Press
Printed in the U.S.A.

# Contents

# Introducing A Retreat With...

Twenty years ago I made a weekend retreat at a Franciscan house on the coast of New Hampshire. The retreat director's opening talk was as lively as a long-range weather forecast. He told us how completely God loves each one of us—without benefit of lively anecdotes or fresh insights.

As the friar rambled on, my inner critic kept up a sotto voce commentary: "I've heard all this before." "Wish he'd say something new that I could chew on." "That poor man really doesn't have much to say." Ever hungry for manna yet untasted, I devalued any experience of hearing the same old thing.

After a good night's sleep, I awoke feeling as peaceful as a traveler who has at last arrived safely home. I walked across the room toward the closet. On the way I passed the sink with its small framed mirror on the wall above. Something caught my eye like an unexpected presence. I turned, saw the reflection in the mirror and said aloud, "No wonder he loves me!"

This involuntary affirmation stunned me. What or whom had I seen in the mirror? When I looked again, it was "just me," an ordinary person with a lower-than-average reservoir of self-esteem. But I knew that in the initial vision I had seen God-in-me breaking through like a sudden sunrise.

At that moment I knew what it meant to be made in the divine image. I understood right down to my size eleven feet what it meant to be loved exactly as I was. Only later did I connect this revelation with one granted to the Trappist monk-writer Thomas Merton. As he reports in *Conjectures of a Guilty Bystander*, while standing all unsuspecting on a street corner one day, he was overwhelmed by the "joy of being...a member of a race in which God Himself became incarnate.... There is no way of telling people that they are all walking around shining like the sun."

As an absentminded homemaker may leave a wedding ring on the kitchen windowsill, so I have often mislaid this precious conviction. But I have never forgotten that particular retreat. It persuaded me that the Spirit rushes in where it will. Not even a boring director or a judgmental retreatant can withstand the "violent wind" that "fills the entire house" where we dwell in expectation (see Acts 2:2).

So why deny ourselves any opportunity to come aside awhile and rest on holy ground? Why not withdraw from the daily web that keeps us muddled and wound? Wordsworth's complaint is ours as well: "The world is too much with us." There is no flu shot to protect us from infection by the skepticism of the media, the greed of commerce, the alienating influence of technology. We need retreats as the deer needs the running stream.

### An Invitation

This book and its companions in the *A Retreat With...* series from St. Anthony Messenger Press are designed to meet that need. They are an invitation to choose as director some of the most powerful, appealing and wise mentors our faith tradition has to offer.

Our directors come from many countries, historical

eras and schools of spirituality. At times they are teamed to sing in close harmony (for example, Francis de Sales, Jane de Chantal and Aelred of Rievaulx on spiritual friendship). Others are paired to kindle an illuminating fire from the friction of their differing views (such as Augustine of Hippo and Mary Magdalene on human sexuality). All have been chosen because, in their humanness and their holiness, they can help us grow in self-knowledge, discernment of God's will and maturity in the Spirit.

Inviting us into relationship with these saints and holy ones are inspired authors from today's world, women and men whose creative gifts open our windows to the Spirit's flow. As a motto for the authors of our series, we have borrowed the advice of Dom Frederick Dunne to the young Thomas Merton. Upon joining the Trappist monks, Merton wanted to sacrifice his writing activities lest they interfere with his contemplative vocation. Dom Frederick wisely advised, "Keep on writing books that make people love the spiritual life."

That is our motto. Our purpose is to foster (or strengthen) friendships between readers and retreat directors—friendships that feed the soul with wisdom, past and present. Like the scribe "trained for the kingdom of heaven," each author brings forth from his or her storeroom "what is new and what is old" (Matthew 13:52).


## The Format

The pattern for each *A Retreat With...* remains the same; readers of one will be in familiar territory when they move on to the next. Each book is organized as a seven-session retreat that readers may adapt to their own schedules or to the needs of a group.

3

Day One begins with an anecdotal introduction called "Getting to Know Our Directors." Readers are given a telling glimpse of the guides with whom they will be sharing the retreat experience. A second section, "Placing Our Directors in Context," will enable retreatants to see the guides in their own historical, geographical, cultural and spiritual settings.

Having made the human link between seeker and guide, the authors go on to "Introducing Our Retreat Theme." This section clarifies how the guide(s) are especially suited to explore the theme and how the retreatant's spirituality can be nourished by it.

After an original "Opening Prayer" to breathe life into the day's reflection, the author, speaking with and through the mentor(s), will begin to spin out the theme. While focusing on the guide(s)' own words and experience, the author may also draw on Scripture, tradition, literature, art, music, psychology or contemporary events to illuminate the path.

Each day's session is followed by reflection questions designed to challenge, affirm and guide the reader in integrating the theme into daily life. A "Closing Prayer" brings the session full circle and provides a spark of inspiration for the reader to harbor until the next session.

Days Two through Six begin with "Coming Together in the Spirit" and follow a format similar to Day One. Day Seven weaves the entire retreat together, encourages a continuation of the mentoring relationship and concludes with "Deepening Your Acquaintance," an envoi to live the theme by God's grace, the director(s)' guidance and the retreatant's discernment. A closing section of Resources serves as a larder from which readers may draw enriching books, videos, cassettes and films.

We hope readers will experience at least one of those memorable "No wonder God loves me!" moments. And we hope that they will have "talked back" to the mentors, as good friends are wont to do.

A case in point: There was once a famous preacher who always drew a capacity crowd to the cathedral. Whenever he spoke, an eccentric old woman sat in the front pew directly beneath the pulpit. She took every opportunity to mumble complaints and contradictions— just loud enough for the preacher to catch the drift that he was not as wonderful as he was reputed to be. Others seated down front glowered at the woman and tried to shush her. But she went right on needling the preacher to her heart's content.

When the old woman died, the congregation was astounded at the depth and sincerity of the preacher's grief. Asked why he was so bereft, he responded, "Now who will help me to grow?"

All of our mentors in *A Retreat With...* are worthy guides. Yet none would seek retreatants who simply said, "Where you lead, I will follow. You're the expert." In truth, our directors provide only half the retreat's content. Readers themselves will generate the other half.

As general editor for the retreat series, I pray that readers will, by their questions, comments, doubts and decision-making, fertilize the seeds our mentors have planted.

And may the Spirit of God rush in to give the growth.

*Gloria Hutchinson*
*Series Editor*
*Conversion of Saint Paul, 1995*

# Getting to Know Our Directors

## Mary of Magdala

At the first sign of dawn on the day after the Sabbath Mary of Magdala hurries to the garden tomb where she has seen Jesus buried. As she walks she weeps. Waves of pain and grief overwhelm her; over and over images of Jesus' trial and crucifixion assault her memory.

Coming into the garden Mary discovers to her surprise that the rock at the tomb's entrance has been rolled away; the tomb is empty. Upset and worried, Mary rushes to tell the other disciples, "They have taken the Lord out of the tomb and I don't know where they have put him."

Peter and John run to look, survey the bleak emptiness of the tomb and go home again. But Mary stays in the garden. She will not be deterred from her purpose. She is determined to find the body of her beloved leader and friend. After he endured so much cruelty, mockery and suffering, she is intent on honoring Jesus' body with the customary burial rites for the dead.

As Mary maintains her vigil outside the tomb she continues to weep and mourn. Everything, everything is lost. Jealous enemies, corrupt leaders, betrayals by close friends—all of these have helped the Roman oppressor unjustly condemn Jesus and put him to a shameful death on the cross. Mary is crushed by her despair, weighed down with hopelessness and helplessness. In these last days she, who has always been able to take charge and minister to others, has been unable to do more than grieve and stand in witness at the site of execution.

Still crying Mary bends over to look inside the tomb. She experiences a vision: two angels in white appear and question her. But Mary is so completely focused upon her mission that she does not panic; she calmly explains her search for Jesus' body and asks for help. As she speaks she is moved to turn herself round toward a human figure she sees nearby. It is Jesus, but at first Mary thinks he is the gardener.

Jesus courteously asks her why she is weeping.

Mary answers and describes her quest.

Then Jesus says, "Mary."

And Mary recognizes him. "Rabboni!" she cries, using her affectionate form of address, "my teacher."

Jesus in response tells Mary not to touch or cling to him here in the garden but to go immediately and tell the brothers that "I am ascending to my Father and your Father, to my God and your God."

Mary goes. She announces to the disciples that she has seen the Lord and gives them the message she was sent to convey.

Confusion? Disbelief? Wonder and surprise? Can we who live twenty centuries later on the other side of the resurrection event begin to imagine these reactions to this good news? Mary's exultant joy upon recognizing Jesus alive is a wholehearted act of triumphant faith. Instantly Mary has been able to assent to a truth that confounds her every expectation. Hopeless and despairing, Mary has come to honor Jesus' dead body in the grave and suddenly she discovers him to be risen, embodied, mysteriously transformed—a human being completely victorious over death. Full of joy Mary sees and believes in Christ's real presence; faithfully she quickly goes to fulfill the charge she has been given.

Ever since this astounding encounter of Mary and Jesus in the garden Christians have longed in joyful anticipation to share fully Mary's experience. We, too, wait to see the Lord face to face. We, too, desire to be called by name and to live with, in and through the risen life of Christ, our savior, our brother, our beloved friend.

And who is this woman who is the first witness to the Resurrection? Who is this first person to be given the mission to go and tell the good news to others? If we think we already know the story of Mary Magdalene we may be in for some surprises.

Many distortions in the historical tradition of the Western Church confound the narrative of Mary of Magdala. She has been called the most slandered saint. During the centuries her identity and her character became confused with other women in the Gospel accounts. Mary of Magdala became identified with Mary of Bethany, or with the penitent harlot who bathed the feet of Jesus with her tears and dried them with her hair. The Eastern Church, by contrast, never identified Mary Magdalene with the fallen woman, and the legends that grew up about Mary in the East portray a strong and powerful woman saint.

Miracles were attributed to Mary in her Western cult, but devotion to the Magdalene also developed extravagant and erotic fables. Often Mary was envisioned as a beautiful, wealthy and sexually passionate courtesan, sometimes depicted as living riotously and sinfully in her castle. Her healing, her conversion, her penitential practices and miracles were elaborated in exotic and romantic fantasies. In Mary Magdalene's story femininity, sexuality, sin and dangerous passion were fused. Today with hindsight we can see that Mary's reputation as the quintessentially sexual woman sinner often paralleled the view of the dangerously seductive nature of all women. In certain ascetic Christian interpretations of the Gospels, attractive women were to be feared because they provoked lustful desires and sexual sins. To avoid temptation women should be segregated and controlled, sometimes even despised for their well-known weaknesses of the flesh.

As myths about Mary multiplied, artists found it irresistible to depict her as the seductive woman who is cured of her sexual demons and passionately repents her sexual sins. Still later, aristocratic ladies vied to be painted in the guise of the beautiful Magdalene. Society artists portrayed Mary in flagrantly suggestive seminude poses. Of one fashionable eighteenth-century picture a wit remarked, "Mmm. Obviously in this picture the Magdalene hasn't repented yet."

Unfortunately, whenever women are thought to be inferior to men, and embodiment is considered generally suspect, women will be lumped together as an alien, dangerous "other." Individual women, like Mary, will find their unique identity swallowed up in some powerful stereotype or archetype of Woman. Yet in a more tolerant mood, perhaps we could admit that these fanciful stories of Mary of Magdala served a purpose. They may have fulfilled that perennial human hunger for glamour, romance and emotional drama. Such fables may even give some backhanded compliment to feminine magnetism and power. And certainly every Christian, male or female, can identify with the deep sorrow and joy of the repentant sinner who is healed.

Today we can begin to correct the distortions of the tradition. But Mary's love for Jesus Christ remains at the core of the real story of Mary of Magdala as saint. Recent biblical scholarship depicts a strong woman with an ardent character who is a leading disciple and an especially beloved friend of Jesus. We can also conclude that Mary has suffered from some serious "demonic" illness that had been healed by the Lord. After being cured, Mary, along with other faithful women, accompanies Jesus from the time of his ministry in Galilee to the final tragedy in Jerusalem.

Mary must have been a woman of some wealth because she and several other socially privileged women are described as ministering to the disciples out of their own resources. As the group of disciples traveled from place to place in Jesus' itinerant ministry, these well-to-do women helped defray expenses. In all four Gospels Mary is always listed first among the women disciples and this position reveals her primary importance. Biblical scholars find new clues to Mary's identity by using new forms of linguistic and cultural analysis. "Mary of Magdala" for instance, is an honorific geographical title that, like "Jesus of Nazareth," testifies to the importance of the person so described. Unlike so many of the other women in the Gospel stories, Mary's name and role is too preeminent to be completely lost by the later scribes who put together the first accounts of Jesus' life.

In every description of the crucifixion Mary is shown as standing among Jesus' most loyal followers and family members. Her steadfast and brave witness is contrasted with the male disciples who out of fear abandon Jesus. Mary's courage, initiative and importance are emphasized again and again in our canonical biblical texts.

Mary's leadership in the early Christian community can also be inferred from her prominence in the surviving noncanonical Christian texts circulating in the late first century. There even exists a "Gospel of Mary." While these texts were eventually rejected by the early Church as inauthentic stories written largely by gnostic heretics, there is no denying the fact that in them Mary of Magdala plays a central role. She is recognized as an intimate friend of Jesus who walked as a companion with him in his ministry; she thereby has the right to take an active part in the dialogues described as taking place between the chief disciples. Another recurring theme in these stories is the conflict between Mary and Peter. She is so often shown challenging Peter (as Saint Paul also did before her) that many scholars have concluded that in all likelihood Mary was the leader of an early Christian community that at some time came into conflict with a group of disciples following Peter.

By any reckoning Mary can now be seen as an influential and leading disciple, an evangelizer and, as many affirm, an apostle. She qualifies as an apostle because she sees the risen Lord and she is sent by name to tell others the Good News. Contrary to many earlier assumptions, it appears that it was possible in late antiquity for some women to take leadership roles.

Certainly in the early Christian communities fluid and flexibly-structured small groups of disciples inspired by the Spirit manifested new and revolutionary freedoms. We see women in Scripture regularly referred to as prophesying and teaching, or being thanked as highly valued coworkers of Paul. Small Church communities are described as meeting in the households of wealthy women patrons, such as Lydia, the seller of purple dyes who became a convert with all her household.

Today scholars agree that certain acts of historical forgetting and selective amnesia can be motivated by later doctrinal conflicts and intrachurch political concerns. As the centuries unfolded and Christianity grew, it became more institutionalized and more assimilated into the hierarchical establishments of the ancient world. Evidence of women's original leadership roles tended to be reinterpreted and discreetly smoothed over in the approved texts. Fortunately, in the twentieth century the character of a strong woman leader such as Mary of Magdala can reemerge from the distortions which minimized her apostolic role and transformed her into a sexual sinner in a romantic fable. Mary more than any other known woman most fully participated in the ministry of Jesus; she experienced the most revolutionary and liberating moment in human history. As the first witness to the Resurrection of the Body, Mary had a unique experience of the importance of embodiment and the power of love in the new creation.

But was Mary herself ever married? We don't know, since no husband or children are mentioned. She is unique in not being identified as anyone's mother, sister, daughter, wife or mistress. In my mind's eye I see Mary of Magdala as a mature but still vigorous widow who runs a successful family business, perhaps in the weaving trade. Magdala, her home town, was a busy port on the sea of Galilee and appears to have been a center of trade, known in particular for its weaving products. Mary can most easily be imagined as a widow because then she would be more likely to have control over her own resources as well as be freer to travel. Since Mary had access to money that she could use to help support the group of disciples, she must have run her business affairs profitably, or she had at least inherited money not subject to family interference. Perhaps because of the early death of a husband and the deaths of any surviving children, Mary had become a free agent. If so, such tragedies might also have precipitated the onset of her illness, or her "possession by seven devils."

And what are we to make of these demons? Later interpreters claimed that these seven demons could be identified with the seven deadly sins! But in first-century Palestinian culture demonic possession was believed to be the explanation for many serious diseases and disabilities, whether mental or physical. I envision Mary as having suffered from attacks of incapacitating depression, a truly debilitating and "demonic" scourge that still afflicts more women than men. From ancient medical texts we know that in the ancient world depressions or melancholias appeared and were recognized as disorders. Anthropological studies also show that women and other marginalized oppressed persons are more likely to be depressed and to be considered possessed.

Whatever the demons that beset Mary, when she encounters Jesus he cures her; after this gift of healing Mary becomes a devoted follower and participates in his mission. Her energies are restored and she is able to follow Jesus as his disciple and close friend—a disciple capable of ministering to Jesus. As a friend of Jesus she, like him, is confident enough to defy convention and to disregard the strict purity taboos which held women to be unclean, polluting and untouchable. Mary's intimate friendship with Jesus is indicated by her greeting of him as Rabboni and by his injunction to refrain from touching him in the garden, as though it would be usual for her to do so. Ironically, this intimate friendship and her leadership among the disciples may be more threatening to many people than the much "safer" characterization of Mary as a female sinner and repentant harlot. In the same way, those on Broadway or in films who have insisted on seeing Mary as the sexual and romantic partner of Jesus, find it more difficult to accept Mary as a strong older female friend who through her abilities can minister to Jesus and actively lead his followers. A daring and wise older woman dedicated to her revolutionary cause can, even today, be a threat. Such women break social taboos and are not easily suppressed.

Mary of Magdala's experience of liberating friendship with the Lord transformed her life and person. Today we can imagine Mary as welcoming those workings of the Spirit in the community which validate women, celebrate human embodiment and encourage equality and friendship between men and women. Over the centuries many antisexual prejudices against the goodness of the body arose among Christians. These strictures have fallen most heavily upon women and laypersons, married or not. Admittedly, the great fourth-century churchman Saint Augustine has contributed his share to fostering negative attitudes toward embodied sexuality. An imagined dialogue between Mary of Magdala and Augustine can only be intriguing.

## Meeting Augustine Again

Augustine comes alive for us when we immerse ourselves in the torrent of his words in his books, sermons, letters and treatises. He has left us five million words of his writing. In his great autobiographical account of his conversion, the *Confessions*, we can meet him in the dramatic and defining crisis of his life. In 384 C.E. Augustine had come to the imperial city of Milan, then the center of the western Roman Empire, intent on pursuing his ambitions for worldly success. Although born in 354 C.E., the son of a relatively poor Roman landowner in a small town in a backward province of Africa, he had gone to Carthage, gained an education and with early success had become filled with expectations for a great career. After a brief sojourn in Rome, Augustine comes to Milan and is finally obtaining a reputation as a brilliant teacher of rhetoric. A young man on the make, Augustine has begun to win patronage in the great sophisticated city; he moves among cultivated pagans and through Christian circles near the court. At last Augustine's long years of hard work and study can make his dream of being appointed an imperial official come true.

But Augustine has become disillusioned with his career and is torn by religious conflicts. In Milan his voracious intellect and quest for truth have encountered the sermons of Ambrose, the learned Catholic bishop. Ambrose has overcome Augustine's skeptical doubts about Christianity. After flirtations with other religious sects and Platonic pagan philosophies, Augustine has become convinced that his mother Monica's fervent Christian faith, the faith of his African childhood, is true. Yet Augustine cannot overcome his ambivalence; he cannot commit himself wholeheartedly to God. The sacrifices entailed seem too onerous. His will is divided, and on one fateful afternoon at home studying and reflecting on his religious troubles, Augustine enters into a violent struggle with himself. In distress he flees into his garden. In his torment he sobs and writhes in distress.

Augustine weeps, he tears his hair, his hands move convulsively; he moans, laments and cries wrack his body. At this extreme moment of crisis he hears children outside singing a rhyming song, "Take and read, Take and read." Augustine listens, picks up his Bible and reads the compelling words of Saint Paul to the Romans warning against sin and enjoining belief in Christ. Instantly Augustine's heart is moved to surrender; his agonized ambivalence melts into a wholehearted assent to God's word and will. Like Mary Magdalene, Augustine in his garden turns his whole self around; in his conversion he instantly receives a wondrous peace and exultant joy. Now he can be baptized; now he will receive the power to change his life.

Augustine gives up his teaching post and with it his ambition for a successful appointment as a governor of a province. In renouncing the world he also gives up plans for an arranged marriage with a young and rich Catholic heiress. He also gives up sex. Sex plays a not inconsiderable part in Augustine's story of his conversion.

From his youth Augustine had been in love with love and tormented by sexual desires. In Carthage he had taken a mistress; he had lived faithfully with her for fifteen years in a second-class marriage arrangement. This was a Roman custom often resorted to by ambitious but poor young men bent on advancement. His mistress had borne him a son, Adeodatus, and they had come with him to Milan.

When the great career and ambitious marriage had finally become possible, Augustine sent his mistress away. As he put it, she "was torn from my side as an impediment to my marriage." She, who is never named, goes back to Africa and vows to remain chaste for the rest of her life. She leaves their beloved son Adeodatus with his father in the Milan household which is run by Monica, Augustine's strongminded mother. Although cultivated Roman gentlemen of the time did not mention their concubines, Augustine reveals in his *Confessions* that upon this loss of his mistress, "my heart which clung to her was torn and wounded til it bled." Apparently to Augustine's surprise, "Nor indeed was the wound healed; only it ceased to burn and throb, and began to fester, and was more dangerous because it was less painful." Since Augustine's sexual needs were so powerful he could not abstain for the two years it would take until his heiress would be old enough to marry. So he took a temporary mistress, admitting sadly that "I was not a lover of wedlock so much as a slave of lust."

Augustine considers that his attachment to sexual pleasure was always immoderate and became fused with his worldly ambition. His sexual enslavement induced his ambivalence toward following God's will. In his judgment, sex and marriage would hold him back from a Christian life. In this view of his vocation he was making a self-assessment as well as following Ambrose and the common opinion of the ascetic teachings of his time. Christian marriage was deemed a good, but virginity and continence, even within marriage, were held up as the better way to holiness. While others might manage a good Christian life in marriage, Augustine judged it would be impossible for him to overcome his "lustful" habits of sexual pleasure. He hints that if his parents had been less ambitious for him and arranged a proper legal marriage in his turbulent youth, things might have been different. Indeed, he always defended the goods of marriage against the attacks of "spiritual" heretics bent on defaming the body. But as an ardent person in everything he did, Augustine determined to dedicate himself to the highest and most certain path to God as he understood it.

When Augustine decided to retire from worldly ambitions, he returned to Africa planning to live quietly in simple retirement with a group of his devout Christian friends. Almost immediately he was drafted to serve as bishop of Hippo. This move meant that he would spend almost four decades of his life, until his death at seventy-six, as an ascetic but actively engaged bishop. He labored heroically to form, inform, protect and lead his unruly flock.

Augustine's magnetic personality and brilliant mind speak to us across the centuries; he impresses us as being intensely passionate, engaging, emotional, toughminded and psychologically acute in his reading of human nature. He wrote and preached vividly because he always responded to the intellectual and emotional upheavals of his time by drawing on his own experiences and reflections. He had to deal with intrachurch conflicts, with heresies among Catholics, with conflicts with pagan thinkers and struggles with officials of the Empire. He even had to deal with violent life-threatening armed bands of local opponents, whether religious or secular. When the shocking news arrived that Rome had been sacked by barbarian invaders, a flood of Roman refugees streamed into Africa. Augustine responded to this crisis with a magnificent attempt in his *The City of God* to understand the meaning of history in the light of Christian faith.

Through his writing Augustine changed the course of the Church and of Western civilization. Yet the great impact he has on us in the twentieth century arises from his modern willingness to look within himself and openly record his private struggles and turbulent feelings. While his own engaging voice sounds in whatever he writes, his most intense personal story is found in his *Confessions*. At forty-three, as a new bishop, Augustine looks back on his youth, his young manhood and his journey to God. In order to help others in their own quest for faith Augustine describes his inner and outer journey to Christianity.

Significantly, in all of his pilgrimage the intensely sociable Augustine is never alone; he is always surrounded by a circle of intimate friends, blood relatives and priests who lived with him in the religious community he formed in his bishop's household. Hospitality, table fellowship and friendship are essential to this man. Perhaps to gain the most characteristic picture of Augustine we might envision him eating and talking with his friends, exploring points, debating, listening and always seeking to learn. He was an ascetic for most of his life, but he remains one of the most charming, delightful and magnetic of personalities. His ardor, his hard work, his love of the Lord and God's creation, his gift for friendship—all can inspire us.

At the time of Augustine's death, hordes of invading

Vandal warbands laid siege to Hippo. War, destruction, torture and martyrdom lay ahead for his city and his Christian flock. Augustine's writings were preserved when his library was carried away to safety in the face of the threat. After Augustine's death the worst happened; the barbarians broke the siege and destroyed the city. Everything that Augustine had labored to build up was torn down when his city and province were sacked. Augustine's Roman world passed away. Only his writing and the example of his passionate life of Christian love and work lived on. It was enough.

## Placing Our Directors in Context

Both Mary Magdalene and Augustine lived in a turbulent time under the military autocracy of Rome. Both saints lived in Mediterranean Roman provinces scarred by peasant rebellions and civil war. First-century Palestine and fourth-century Africa were examples of oppressive social and economic systems; they were brutally unjust societies in which the rich became richer and the poor were being increasingly ground down into destitution. Lawless violence and the violent suppression of dissent were commonplace, and both societies were drifting toward rebellion, war and military devastation.

Mary of Magdala lived in a complicated time and place that has fascinated all those seeking to understand Jesus of Nazareth. Historians are reassessing first-century Palestine and first-century Judaism, as new archaeological discoveries and methods of inquiry develop. A sophisticated Greco-Hellenistic urban society of Greeks, Romans and Jews existed in Palestine along with, or on the backs of, a Jewish agrarian peasant society. All of these groups lived under the yoke of the Roman conquest with its iron authority.

Trade routes went through Palestine from Eastern civilizations on the way to Mediterranean seaports. Diverse religious influences from both East and West influenced Jewish religious life. Turbulent inner divisions marked the Judaism of the time; there were ascetic sects such as the Essenes along with violent Jewish rebels whose revolt against Rome had recently been suppressed.

It was a violent and confusing time, a time building up to another Jewish revolt that would again be suppressed by Roman legions who this time would destroy the temple at Jerusalem. Many teachers, prophets and itinerant healers could flourish in such a period of unrest. The early Christian groups at first were one among many religious associations that flourished, primarily in the cities of the Empire.

Later, when persecutions of the Christians began, it took great courage to be a follower of Jesus of Nazareth and to become one of those persons who "turned the world upside down." Eventually the Church triumphed over the Roman Empire, but at a tremendous price. The blood of martyrs watered the seedbeds of the Church.

Augustine lived three centuries later in a nominally Christianized Roman Empire; he thought of himself as a thoroughly civilized Roman citizen. While he lived in a backwater African province, he lived there as a poorer member of the civilized Roman gentry who spoke Latin and looked down upon the Punic natives laboring on the great estates known as Rome's breadbasket. By the fourth century, Christians were no longer persecuted and the Empire was officially Christian. In reality pagan culture still had enormous influence and many Christians were only superficially converted.

Poor young African gentry like Augustine, who came from ambitious Latin-speaking Roman families, would be pushed to succeed in the larger world of the Empire. They were given a narrow but intensive education in the Latin classics. The most cultivated and educated elites would also learn Greek and have access to the Greek classics. Augustine knew little Greek, but he was a master of Latin literature and the skills of rhetoric and debate.

African Christianity also had a distinctive character; it was an extremely superstitious, legalistic, primitive and contentious faith full of violent sects and heretical parties contending for supremacy. Trances, demonic possessions, raucous celebrations, sexual infidelity, slavery and alcoholism afflicted the Christian congregations. Violent bands of heretics might roam the countryside destroying churches and threatening the lives of priests and bishops.

These increasingly violent parties within African Christianity were symptomatic of the breakdown of government within the Roman Empire. The emperors were already hardpressed from the Persian empire in the East and were no longer able to protect their western territories from the pressure of the northern barbarian armies. During Augustine's lifetime barbarian troops sacked Rome; Rome the eternal city, the symbol of all civilization, fell and was pillaged.

As historians have noted, Augustine started out as a citizen of the late Roman Empire and ended his life as a denizen of the medieval world which was given birth by the dark ages of the barbarian invasions.

## For Reflection

*Augustine and Mary of Magdala can serve as wonderful guides for today's Christians seeking to become mature lovers of God and others. Both saints have a genius for giving and receiving the gift of friendship. They are leaders and exemplars of holiness who have thrilled and magnetically attracted people throughout the centuries. As passionate spirits they don't hold back; they live to the fullest in wholehearted love and celebrate the gift and grace of embodied existence. Each of these great hearts experienced healing and conversion in their encounters with Christ's love; they seek to be transformed in the new creation of the kingdom.*

*Both Mary and Augustine are intense seekers of the truth. Mary broke with the conventions of her time and followed Christ. Before and after the Resurrection she is able to turn toward the new and go out to embrace a revolutionary path of discipleship. Augustine is a man on fire to know and understand more fully the truth and love he has experienced. He was in constant conversation with others and with himself.*

*Now we can imagine him in dialogue with Mary of Magdala and with ourselves. In the company of Christ, the eternal conversation goes on forever between friends. We can gladly turn to these two personalities when we, in our own turbulent times, seek to reflect on love, sex and marriage.*

## Notes

[1] Augustine, *Confessions*, trans. R.S. Pine-Coffin (New York: Penguin Classics, 1961), Book VI, 15, p. 131.

[2] Ibid.

[3] Ibid.

[4] Ibid.

# DAY ONE
## Passion's Transforming Power

### Introducing Our Retreat Theme

Have Christians adequately reflected on all the ways they can glorify God in their marriages? No, not really, and the silence surrounding sexuality has been even more complete. Few married persons contribute to the discourse on Christian marriage. And officially canonized married saints (what few exist) have never written about the intimate sexual dimension of their marital life together. Whether this near-total silence comes from a desire for privacy or a sense of bewilderment, a void remains. Most of today's Christians might agree that we need more reflection on good marriages in our changing society and more nurturing of married people within the Catholic Church.

Christianity correctly and wisely insists that human sexuality flourishes in permanent mutual commitments. Those who discount the bonds of fidelity end up inflicting harm upon themselves and others. Men, women, children and families suffer when marriage commitments falter. The goods accompanying lasting marriages and stable families accrue to individuals, as well as to the larger society.

Most Christians today also agree with Vatican II's teachings which affirm that the two ends of marriage, unity and procreation, are equally valuable and complementary. Happily, too, an array of council documents, papal encyclicals, bishops' statements and treatises by theologians have finally and definitively affirmed that the vocation of Christian marriage is equal to that of dedicated celibacy. No more second-class citizenship for the married laity! Faithful married love is extolled frequently in the modern Church, and long-married couples receive beautiful scrolls of commendation—along with the praise and applause of all.

But how does sexual embodiment fit into the idealized vision of Christian married love that is affirmed and extolled? We hear less about living a good and passionate Christian sexual life in a friendship of equals. After all, most traditional forms of spirituality were created by celibates to meet the needs of other celibates. In the past, married people seeking holiness might be instructed to emulate the celibate pattern of sexual continence, sacrifice, detachment and devotion. So where do married people learn about a conjugal path to wholeness and holiness? This retreat provides one thoughtful response.

To explore questions of marital sexuality and loving friendship in our retreat we are going to call upon two passionate friends of God, Mary Magdalene and Augustine. They enthusiastically affirmed Christ's power to liberate and transform our human nature. They know that mind, heart, will and body must be renewed in the new creation of the Resurrection. These two greathearted followers of the Lord were persistent seekers and doers of the truth. As we envision them in dialogue we can all, together in the communion of saints, seek new truths about love and passion in Christian marriage.

## Opening Prayer

Lord, help us to believe that you have made us for yourself so we can worship you as the God of Love Who Is. Your goodness and truth make us desire to give you thanks and praise. We offer you our times of love and joy in one another, secure in the knowledge that in loving those we see we love you as well. May your good gifts of sexual delight dilate our hearts and help us to understand your love for us and your wondrous creation. Let us grow through love for one another into a full realization of our bodily resurrection in Christ.

# RETREAT SESSION ONE

*Sit up straight, quicken your breathing and stir up your mind and heart for some imaginative confrontation. A dialogue between Mary Magdalene and Augustine means an encounter between two strong personalities of great charm, charisma, competence and courtesy; but each saint also displayed a steely determination. Sparks may fly.*

**Mary:** My dear Augustine. How I admire your work and your heroic life devoted to serving God. You write of the joyful allure and the healing powers of God's love as no one else ever has.

**Augustine:** Honored lady, you are too gracious in your praise. But let me begin by offering any apologies due you for anything offensive I may have written about you in my commentaries on Scripture. You must forgive those of us who in our day were struggling with inadequate scholarly tools, trying as best we could to understand the saving

Word of God.

**Mary:** I do forgive you. Of course I noted with a smile that you thought it a good thing that the risen Jesus first appeared to me, a woman, so that Christians should not "justly despise" women! But since you said the same thing about God favoring the Virgin Mary and thereby taking away women's shame, how can I complain?

But I was offended when commentators saw me as a totally different type of woman than Mary, the Lord's dear mother. How much damage has been done to women by that old prejudiced dichotomy of the good versus the bad woman, the holy virgin versus the sinful sexual woman as whore! In fact, I was not the same woman as the repentant prostitute described in the Gospels, and the seven demons I suffered from were never the seven deadly sins.

**Augustine:** But I never said that you were the same woman as the prostitute or a notorious sinner.

**Mary:** Yes, I know. But like other Christian thinkers of your time you believed Eve to be the cause of the fall, and so judged the daughters of Eve to be by nature weaker than the male sex. For you, women's supposed inferiority justified their being subject to male authority. Before we begin to debate these interpretations perhaps we could admit from the start that women, from Eve onward, have been misinterpreted, misunderstood and slandered.

Of course, our Lord too was always misunderstood; and he warned us that, as his disciples, we should expect to be treated as he was. Surely you, too, have suffered calumny from your opponents who attacked you as you worked to build up the Church.

**Augustine:** Ah yes, I have been involved in so many bitter conflicts and disputes in my time. But I was also blessed, of course, with the encouragement of a good mother, a father who sacrificed for my studies and a host of stimulating friends and spiritual mentors in the Lord. If only my worldly ambition and dissolute youth had not led me to waste so much of my young adulthood in the snares of sin and error. How grateful I am that the Lord, the Life of My Life, came and found me. Christ, the great physician, healed me; and he continues to transform human beings into his likeness.

**Mary:** Yes, I, too, was healed by the Lord and rescued from my "demons," which were devastating bouts of mental illness. I was hopeless and helpless, overwhelmed by despair when I met Jesus in that dusty Galilean town. Miraculously, I was healed by his words and his touch, and my life was given back to me. And I was not the only one. Over and over I saw Jesus moved with pity and tender compassion for the crowds who came to him for help; he healed and comforted those who sought his aid. How privileged I was to see with my own eyes the gracious kindness and glory of the Lord with us. And most wonderfully in the end I was given my life back a second time when I beheld Christ's victorious resurrection. We have been saved from the nothingness of extinction. Surely you and I can together praise the precious gifts of a new and abundant life that we have received in a redeemed creation.

**Augustine:** Yes, yes, I join you in giving praise for the blessings of all nature. I have written much in grateful celebration of our God's wondrous creation: I praise the sun and stars, and all the cultural marvels created by human talents. I sing of country landscapes, the arts, the animals and even the smallest insects, which show forth

God's beauty, goodness and gracious kindness. God's creation is good, very, very good.

And although my critics hardly ever notice it, I have also sung the wonders of the human body for all its skillful ingenuities and beauties of development, and even more for its amazing hidden workings which the medical men of my day have found as they explore its inner mysteries. I have much admired the work of a wise physician friend of mine who read and understood the works of the physician Hippocrates. This was the same friend who helped me overcome the superstitions of astrology toward which, alas, I was for so long attracted.

To my way of thinking all reasoned study of science and the arts helps us to discover more about the divine Wisdom and the Word who creates and sustains this wonder-filled world of order, joy and delight. Everything that exists must participate in the goodness and power of God, who proclaims "I am who am."

**Mary:** You are so true to our Lord and the Hebrew Scriptures when you proclaim the marvels of the creation. But, hearing your paeans of praise, I am brought up short and puzzled by one aspect of your thinking. Why do you seem to make such an exception of human sexuality when you tell of God's goodness displayed in creation? Surely the joys and fruitfulness of married sexuality must include sexual pleasure as a primary gift of God to humankind. Loving sexual union is the embodiment of the loving bond between husband and wife and increases a couple's love. What greater act of love of another can there be than the unity resulting from the passionate giving and receiving of sexual love?

**Augustine:** No, no. Never. I cannot accept passionate sexual desire and sexual pleasure as a positive good, even when enacted in Christian marriage for the purpose of producing children. Since the fall of our race sexual desire and intercourse is always a sign and a mark of the death brought by sin. Sexuality can only be turned to an acceptable good end when used well in marriage to procreate. Sexual intercourse in marriage can be better than lustfulness; it is better to marry than to burn, and much better to marry than commit fornication or adultery.

Why do you think that almost all of the Christian world I knew judged virginity and continence dedicated to the Lord to be a far better and more perfect way to holiness? Because sexual intercourse always is tainted by immoderate passionate desires that are not subject to the control of the will. Indeed, when married persons can mutually agree to practice continence in marriage it is a very good thing; if, that is, they both give their consent. And it is far worthier if a couple agrees to abstain from sex when they are still in their prime—rather than when they are so old that they become naturally continent.

**Mary:** Naturally continent? Intercourse always tainted by passion? Oh my dear Augustine, I have so many problems with these views of yours. I cannot understand why continence should be good for married Christians if marriage and sexuality are good creations of God, and surely this is the message we are given in Genesis. Jesus, too, taught that marriage was a good created by God from the beginning; and he implicitly blessed marriage at the wedding feast of Cana. Over and over he used positive images from marriage and family life to describe the Kingdom. He spoke of himself as a bridegroom, echoing Old Testament images. Just think of how many of his parables take their themes from marital and family life.

I can personally attest to the fact that the Jesus I knew was completely at ease with his own sexuality and with that of others; Jesus accepted himself and was accepting of women, as well as his married friends and family. Remember the many women friends he visited and the women disciples like myself that he travelled with. I saw him heal so many women, how tender and loving he was—as when he bent over Peter's mother-in-law's bed and healed her fever. He often healed through touch, you know—touching even those who were thought to be impure, such as bleeding women, prostitutes, lepers, the ill and corpses. Surely his revolutionary acceptance of women, children, the ill and the dying attests to his comfort with our human bodily existence. He came eating and drinking, loving and accepting every body. In this, he was constantly shocking his own followers!

**Augustine:** But Jesus also taught that some should be eunuchs for the Kingdom of heaven. He praised those who gave up marriage and family and homes in order to follow him. Surely his own celibate example counts as a message for us that sexuality is suspect.

**Mary:** No, no. Many Jewish prophets and men of God were celibate, like John the Baptizer, in order to be free not only to travel and preach but also to take risks when they denounced the sins of the powerful against the poor. In this, as in everything else, Jesus was fulfilling our Jewish inheritance of affirming the goodness of all human life in all its dimensions. But what, pray tell, do you make of Jesus' praise of marriage? And what do you do with the affirmation of sexual pleasure in our Hebrew tradition? Think of the Song of Songs. I protest your distortions of the gospel by your negative focus on sexual desire.

**Augustine:** My dear lady, let me clarify my position. I, too, believe sexual pleasure in marriage was meant to be a good gift from God. Before the fall Adam and Eve would have had a controlled and voluntary sexual concord in paradise, but after man's proud rebellion of the human will against God, involuntary sexual desires become a perversely deformed wound of human nature. The involuntary lusts of sexual desires, like the involuntary death of the body, are the fitting punishment for a rebellion of the will. Sexual desire's excessively immoderate driving force creates havoc within humankind. It is an all-powerful pervasive drive and so the most subject to sinful passions of all human capacities—all because of its involuntary, uncontrollable nature. Unavoidably, sexual sin accompanies each conception of a new human life by sexual intercourse; and so original sin and our wounded human nature are passed from generation to generation.

Worst of all, as I found in my own lustful youth, sexual passions ensnare the soul in attachments to the flesh and this world here below. I long hesitated to become a Christian because, enchained in my lusts, I could not forgo my sexual pleasures.

Surely you must grant that sexual passion is the strongest of all pleasures and that human lust, like other forms of greed, is difficult to tame and master. Even as an old man I was troubled by lustful thoughts and dreams.

But, mind you, I do not make sexual passion the only sinful enemy arising from rebellious pride that we must fight on our path to holiness. Indeed, any sensual pleasure such as eating, or drinking, or even delights of the eye, such as when I am beguiled into watching a dog chase a hare in the countryside or a lizard catch flies, or even by listening to music—all of these distractions can make me lose my self-control and impede me from attending to God, who alone is my true light.

Inordinate sexual passion or immoderate love of a

mistress, spouse, or of a mother or a child, or of a friend, or (my own worst sin) the desire to be praised, admired and loved, these strong worldly attachments will keep the soul from a wholehearted love of God.

**Mary:** O my dear Augustine, your own unfortunate experiences with sexuality are not everyone's experience. And how needlessly you berate yourself for your attachments to those persons you love. Your ardent love of your friends and your family members is one of the most attractive things about you. I see that these attachments bring you to God and teach you about loving God. You seem so mistaken when you imply that God Who Is Love can be diminished by a human being's attachment to another human being. God commands us to love one another; we are told to love God and our neighbor as our self. Christ always loved his own and ministered to them, as well as loving his neighbors. His love for everyone was so excessive and immoderately passionate that it led to his dying for us.

As I listen to you it appears that you seem to be operating with a belief in the scarcity or limited view of loving; if I love my wife or husband then I cannot love God as much, or if I love my son or mother it will take away from the amount of love I can give to God. But God's gift of love is limitless and can only abound. Within the Christian life of the Kingdom, it is as within the Trinity, when a human being gives love and receives love from another, this love creates and begets ever more loving of God and neighbor.

I think your basic misunderstanding seems to be that you think that loving other human beings or the beauties of the world will somehow distract or compete with your loving God or that other loves offend him. But such loving comes from God. After all God dwells within the beloved person too. We disciples were told this message by the Lord repeatedly. Love others as I have loved you. Jesus told us that when we feed and clothe and give water to our thirsty neighbor, or wash each other's feet we do this to him as well, to the Christ living within that human person. Why should not loving and pleasing my spouse be a way of loving God? Erotic love is even better than feeding, washing or clothing another; it can be an especially intense form of charity. When you speak of your hope of God to be "melted by the fire of your love and fused into one with you,"[1] you could be describing the grace of sexual loving in marriage.

**Augustine:** But I am decidedly *not* doing any such thing! I wish my love of God to be singleheartedly, passionately, absolutely focused upon the Eternal Immutable One. When I love my neighbor or the beauties of the world it is in order to rise and *ascend* through that love to the higher love of God. While the body is good and wonderful, it must serve as a good servant; our bodies can never be as valuable as the gift of our rational mind or soul. The body and soul are united as in a good marriage, and the mind must rule and govern—just as a man must govern his wife. The body is corruptible and is dying. Only the mind and soul can understand and consciously rise to God who is Eternal Unchanging Spirit. What, I ask you, what understanding of God can be gained by sexual passion which overcomes all the mind's rational powers?

**Mary:** I hold that sexual passion, like abounding grace, can be accepted as a sign of God's good and bountiful giving, *especially* when it rises to an ecstasy that overcomes self-consciousness.

Marital sexual passion shows forth the power and delight of God's love and joy. In sex we can worship the

Lord with gladness. We are told that God delights in his creation and a sexual delight in one's own spouse, or for that matter the passionate love of one's own child, gives Christians an understanding of God's love and delight in each of us.

Also sexual pleasure in marriage prefigures heaven's happiness and the heavenly marriage of the lamb in the Resurrection. So this is what a resurrected body joined with others may be like! In sexual passion we understand what it is to receive and enjoy blessed fulfillment. Such experiences, or epiphanies, rouse us out of our dull everyday torpor and inspire us to understand what God's love and Christ's passion to save us is all about.

Can experiences of sexual desire and love transform the personality? Yes, because sexual passion helps us understand love and confirms that an invisible world and invisible powers exist beyond everyday ordinary appearances. Sometimes this vision can be a comic and merry one. Imagining that people we know and see walking around so calmly enjoyed desire and passion opens our eyes to the hidden dimensions of life in society.

**Augustine:** Please, dear lady, have you no decorum or sense of shame?

**Mary:** Oh, you require Roman decorum, do you? No, dear friend, my life has not been that of an aristocratic Roman gentlewoman. Nonetheless, I am quite sure that my experiences have taught me what is truly shameful and what is not. I would even go so far as to affirm that marital love can heal any false shame over our bodies that we may have. Sexual loving that completely accepts embodied intimacy also heals the body's sense of incompleteness and vulnerability.

Marital sexuality is important in the sacramental

union in which two become one; it expresses and makes real the union of wills in vowed friendship. Sexual joy and pleasure can be an experience of that "region of unfailing plenty"[2] you have glimpsed. Can't you see that sexual ecstasy is one way to worship and enter the courts of the Lord with praise? But I see that I am offending you again. Let us then agree to be silent for a while and continue our conversation tomorrow.

**Augustine:** Yes, I am fairly scandalized to hear from you ideas that are similar to those of that heretic Julian of Eclanum that I fought against so fiercely in my old age. I can only assure you that since the fall, sexual desire more than anything else distracts and diverts attention from prayer and worship. Sexuality endangers virtue and is at the root of much sin. In or out of marriage nothing is more out of control or rebels against the will more than our sexual desires.

**Mary:** So you say. But enough for now. Until tomorrow.

## For Reflection

- *How have I truly accepted and celebrated God's creation as very good?*

- *How have I demonstrated my gratitude for my embodied human nature and looked upon my sexuality as a gift from God? When I have not done so, what were the circumstances that should be avoided?*

- *How can I show that love for my spouse, and for other human beings made in the image of God and within whom Christ dwells, is a way of loving God?*

- *When have I experienced and celebrated passion's transforming power?*

- *Is it possible that my passionate desire for my spouse might enable me to experience more fully God's passionate desire for me? Why or why not?*

## Closing Prayer

*Augustine's great prayers of devotion will close our retreat sessions.*

Eternal Truth, true Love, beloved Eternity—all, my God you are, and it is to you that I sigh by night and day. When first I knew you you raised me up so that I could see that there was something to be seen, but also that I was not yet able to see it. I gazed on you with eyes too weak to resist the dazzle of your splendour. Your light shone upon me in its brilliance, and I thrilled with love and dread alike. I realized that I was far away from you. It was as though I were in a land where all is different from your own and I heard your voice calling from on high, saying "I am the food of full-grown men. Grow and you shall feed on me. But you shall not change me into your own substance, as you do with the food of your body. Instead you shall be changed into me."[3]

## Notes

[1] *Confessions*, Book XI, p. 279.

[2] Ibid., Book IX, 10, p. 197.

[3] Ibid., Book VII, 10, p. 147.

# Day Two
## Keeping Desire Going

### Coming Together in the Spirit

In the comic film *Baby Boom* a superachieving young single executive (Diane Keaton) is transformed by the sudden advent in her life of an orphaned baby. While viewers delight in watching her hilarious progress from cool work-obsession to emotional warmth, we're also treated to a comic micro-lesson on sex. B.B., or before baby, Diane Keaton and her equally driven live-in male partner are seen lying in bed reading their respective business briefs. At a murmured signal they promptly take off their glasses, put aside their papers and turn off the light. The clock reads 10:31 at fade out.

As the light returns, the clock reads 10:37; the bedmates have their glasses back in place and have resumed the perusal of their paperwork. How could such a briskly efficient sexual exchange do justice to a couple's potential for playful adoration or mutual delight in their union? Neither a sense of vulnerability, nor a delight in leisured celebration mark this calculated coupling.

Not to worry. Since this is Hollywood we can be assured of a happier future for our heroine. A.B., or after baby, when the adorable infant girl has been adopted and a gentler, kinder Ms. Keaton moves to an apple farm in the country, life takes a turn for the better. She has dumped her rigid boyfriend who refuses to embrace fatherhood and does not choose to risk his career by getting closer to nature. Too bad. By embracing motherhood our executive's virtue is enlarged and immediately rewarded. In short order she (1) devises a successful applesauce business and (2) meets a ruggedly handsome carpenter who will become her ideal mate.

Flash forward to a scene wherein our heroine is talking to her friend on the phone after a night of love; she coyly admits she has not gotten a wink of sleep. Voila! With the love of a baby and apples by the dozens, our young woman gets in touch with her true nature and finds passionate fulfillment. The handsome couple will marry, have many more babies and live happily ever after. Sexuality blossoms with the good life.

True enough. But unfortunately in the real world no one can take care of a baby or run a successful business without adequate sleep. Granted, sexual passion may suffer from the endemic overwork and stress endured by most Americans, but this doesn't change the fact that work is necessary for survival and self-fulfillment. Work, like the art of sexual communion and intimate marital friendship, takes a lot of time and loving care in order to bear fruit. So how can you keep the demands of work and love in balance? This is a perennial modern puzzle that is not resolved by going to the movies.

## Defining Our Thematic Context

Contrary to ascetic stereotypes that marital morality is endangered by rampant sexual indulgence, the opposite is more often true. Married lovers can have more trouble finding enough time and space and energy to tend to their loving sexual intimacy. As one shrewd Benedictine monk describes his view of the ironic situation in the modern Church, "The most dramatic, indeed comic, instance of cross-purposes between the Vatican and the married, is that the Vatican sees the problem as one of curbing desire, whereas the married know that the problem is to keep desire going, which means to keep it growing, which means deepening."[1]

Married laypersons don't need to be warned against "unbridled lust," but against too firmly bridled neglect of their sexuality. Feeding the fires of sexual love and devotion takes energy and commitment. In a long marriage people may go through many ups and downs and cycles of adjustment, but embodied wholehearted sexual loving is a central way that married people grow in unity.

The bond between persons is strengthened by the mutual immersion into the joyful waters, and it is even more wonderful when there can be a final plunge into the liberating tide of orgasmic passion. The challenge of marital sexuality is to grow more mutually sensitive, more sexually wholehearted and attuned, more able intently to focus love and desire upon the beloved spouse.

## Opening Prayer

Lord, make us more passionate in our marital loving. Enkindle the fires of sexual desire and let us ardently seek to give and receive pleasure without fear or shame. We give thanks for all your gifts of body, mind and heart which rise up within us without the effort of will. Help us be more enchanted by your beauty as we exult and abound in your gifts to us of love.

# Retreat Session Two

**Mary:** Back to our dialogue, dear Augustine, and to differing views. Don't you ever suspect that despite your protestations, you still assume that the body and sexuality are unclean, or polluted in some way? Your references to virgins not being "violated" by marital sexuality appear to give away your feelings of disgust for the body's functions. And you speak so often of "unclean," sexual acts "too vile to be mentioned."[2] Have you not succumbed to the heretical view of bodies and bodily needs as shameful and the source of evil?

**Augustine:** No, no. As I have repeatedly affirmed, I see the human body as part of God's beautiful creation. We are partly our bodies as well as our souls and everything that exists or has being can only exist in a good God Who Is. Evil and sin can only come from the rebellion of the will against God's standards.

But the creation must remain ordered and humankind must not let a perverted will deform God's order. Order, and peace as the tranquillity of order, can exist only when the body does not rebel against reason or the soul. Since sexual desire and intercourse cannot be controlled in a reasonable, moderate, temperate manner, I think the great pagan philosophers were correct to point out that human beings appropriately feel shame at their loss of control in sexual acts. This shame makes people generally cover their genitals, and when having sexual intercourse people seek to be hidden.

Christians along with wise pagans must acknowledge the dangers lurking within bodily sexual passion in our fallen human nature. Some medical authorities of my time compare sexual orgasm to an epileptic fit and consider it definitely harmful to one's health. Yes, for many reasons, the great stoic philosophers and our contemporary Christian saints correctly preach a necessary detachment from all sexual desires.

All human attachments enslave our minds and sap the strength of our will to ascend to higher things of the Spirit. The things of the body are changeable and corruptible, and while corruptible things in creation are good, they can never be as good as the higher realms of mind and spirit which participate in divine immutability and self-sufficiency. Our bodies will be raised in the resurrection but the divine soul can exist without a body.

**Mary:** Oh dear, your phrase "peace as the tranquility of order," always reminds me of nothing so much as death—a corpse manifests perfect order and peace. And this talk of immutability sounds odd for the God who says to us Christians, "Behold I make all things new." The God of Israel is alive and responsive; he leads the people night and day into new paths and speaks to Job out of the whirlwind.

And can souls exist without bodies? We Jews always think of living people as an undivided whole, we have few words for these more abstract divisions of human beings into body or mind or soul. It even sounds strange to me when you, dear Augustine, speak of the soul and body as existing in married concord as though they could somehow really be separate entities. For us, the whole person is referred to by the word "heart." Jesus always told us that it was the things that come forth from the heart that count with God. Nothing external or physical that goes into the person can pollute you.

I remember with joy that when we walked with the Lord he freed us from fear of ritual pollutions and impurities that supposedly arise from contact with

43

unclean bodily things. I can testify that Jesus never thought of women as unclean, even the touch of the woman hemorrhaging menstrual blood only earned his public notice and praise for her faith in his power to heal her. He never hesitated to eat and drink with sinners or to touch the sick, the leprous or the dead, all deemed to be ritually polluting by some religious people. Bodily emissions were also thought to be unclean, but not for the Lord. In fact, I once saw Jesus mix his saliva with mud and apply this paste to a blind man's eyes in order to heal him. No, Jesus never put people or their bodies into shameful separate categories of untouchability or uncleanness. Jesus healed us all from feeling shame in our bodily natures.

So why do you think human beings ought to be ashamed in their embodied sexuality when it is a good capacity created by God? By the way, shame about one's genitals is not even universally the case as you claim. Surely you remember seeing pagan Greeks and Romans going to the baths; they thought nothing of freely walking about nude in front of their servants and friends. You even report that occasion in your adolescence when you went to the baths with your father. He joked and laughed at your involuntary erection. He saw it as proof of your new manhood and was glad that he could look forward to having grandchildren. Now as a sensitive youth, that may have embarrassed and shamed you, but it certainly doesn't prove your argument for the universality of bodyshame. You seem to think that all humankind, beginning with Adam, must have the same experiences as the adolescent Augustine.

Moreover, I do not believe that shame is the reason people seek sexual privacy. People desire privacy for their sexual relationships because they want to concentrate on their lovemaking and not be distracted in their intimacy by interruptions or intrusions from others. Privacy also gives you a sense of safety. Passionate feelings completely capture and focus attention so that they can make you oblivious and potentially vulnerable to external dangers. When you are so enthralled you cannot be vigilant or anxious.

Indeed, being transported and enchanted is one of the great gifts of sexual loving. Naturally people seek quiet leisured privacy for intercourse, just as they do for intimate intense conversations. Think of how we follow the Lord's instructions to retire to our closeted chamber when we wish to pray intimately and passionately to God. That retreat to privacy doesn't signal a sense of shame, does it?

Why, dear Augustine, can you not admit that our Lord, by his victory over death in the Resurrection, completely vindicated the goodness of all of our embodied human existence, including sexual desires, pleasure and passionate fulfillment?

**Augustine:** But Mary, why can't *you* admit that Christ knew that sexuality could be misused in sinful thoughts, desires and acts? Christ knew what was in man and recognized the power of evil and sin. He warned against lusting after a women in your heart and told the adulterous woman to go and sin no more.

**Mary:** Yes, after he saved her from being stoned to death by the mob. When Jesus told those accusing the poor woman that only those who had no sin should throw the first stone, I saw him bend down and write the symbols for the Ten Commandments in the sand. That reminder of all of God's commandments to his people made even the most vengeful and self-righteous men present recognize that they too were sinners. They slunk away, beginning with the eldest. Now there was an example of our human capacity to feel shame working in a good way!

But to get back to your question about evil, yes, of course Jesus recognized its power and destructiveness. He knew what was likely to be his fate as God's beloved Word to a sinful world. Surely every good human activity can become corrupted—sex, religion, language, family life. I agree with you, Augustine, when you say that all sinful acts arise from rebelling against God's goodness when humans harden their hearts into stone.

Yet, Jesus hardly spent much time warning us against the dangers of sexual sin when compared to his admonitions against hypocrisy, pride, love of money and injustice to the poor. But even if we grant the existence of grievous sexual sins, this can hardly mean that all acts of sexual love in marriage must be corrupted or dangerous. Quite the contrary.

**Augustine:** But surely, dear lady, you admit that sexual desire and sexual acts attach us to this world. They arise against the will and carry away the mind's rational self-control. They drag persons down into gross insensibility.

**Mary:** Why down? Why gross? Your levels of hierarchies and other such philosophical notions of human beings seem so dualistic and artificial. Knowing the Ten Commandments and the Lord's teaching on marriage, I agree that sexuality must always be ordered to the whole person, to all of a person's goals for a good life.

But surely it is no more difficult to direct one's sexuality than it is to govern one's tongue. Jesus commanded us to avoid harming another by hurtful words; remember that he used much stronger language for someone calling another "Thou fool," than he did to the woman taken in adultery. Pride appears far worse than sinful sexual lapses.

I cannot grant that because sexual desires and acts can be involuntary and are sometimes difficult to direct that they are therefore degrading or degraded.

**Augustine:** So you say.

**Mary:** Let me try to convince you using some of your own ideas. I have been impressed with how shrewdly you have noted the mysteriousness of our involuntary workings of memory. You note that somehow, we know not how, we are able to become conscious of things which may be mysteriously absent at one moment but not forever lost. Inspirations and creative insights of all sorts simply well up into consciousness without our willing them. Indeed, when the Spirit blows where it freely wills and fills human beings so that they prophesy, they are not exercising voluntary self-control.

So if the involuntary workings of the mind and memory and spirit are gifts from a good God, why should not involuntary sexual desires and pleasures also be good gifts?

You, the great champion of God's gift of grace which we do not earn, or control, or deserve, should be able to see that the involuntary pleasures we can experience in a good marriage can be as good a dimension of sexuality as procreation. It is a good thing to be open to melting in the heat of love and ecstasy. Who exercises self-control in ecstatic joy? Remember David leaping and dancing naked before the ark of the Lord in joyful celebration. Remember the Song of Songs which after many beautiful sensuous descriptions of sexual love enjoins the lovers, "Eat, friends, drink, and be drunk with love" (Song of Songs, 5:1).

When other mystics and ecstatics praise God's love

47

and sweetness in sexual or nuptial terms they, too, are recognizing and celebrating the primary giftedness of the experiences of erotic love. Other forms of loving ascribed to God, such as that of a mother or a father's tender care, also gain their power from our original experiences of tender embodied human loving.

So, dear friend, forget those ideals of sober self-controlled *gravitas* and puritanical *severitas* you soaked up from the Roman writers and stoic philosophers you so admire. Try to envision that the ardor you experience in divine love might be God's will for human loving.

**Augustine:** Perhaps I have been too much influenced by my ascetic Christian guides and by my Latin mentors. You must remember, however, that from my youth the great Romans and their classics exemplified the epitome of civilized behavior for me. When I first read Cicero he opened up to me the serious life of philosophy and wisdom. He and the other great Platonist philosophers freed me from the crude materialism of my provincial African cultural milieu.

There is also much to be said in defense of traditional Roman ideals of self-control. Just think how much the world and the churches have suffered from passion and the violence of unrestrained evil emotions and desires. My congregations of Christians have been constantly endangered by excesses of sexual passion, drunkenness, intemperate greed and violence of all kinds. My superstitious Christian flocks continue to resort to magic, trances and raucous celebrations that end in near riots. Their behavior convinces me of the dangers of losing rational control of one's self and of the excesses of emotions.

Sexual desires and lusts produce some of the worst evils in our fallen world. You in your time witnessed the murder of John the Baptist as a victim of Herod's lust and his wife's anger for being criticized for her dissolute life. More recently, when Rome was sacked by the barbarians, we received as refugees here in Africa many nuns who were raped. Violence against women arises from shameful lusts. All slaves' bodies are considered to be the sexual property of their masters. One old man I know of, who at eighty-three had always lived an exemplary life, suddenly purchased a lyre girl for his sexual pleasure.

I seriously doubt that my own youthful sexual bondage was a unique case. I know of too many other dreadful excesses of passion that are destroying our decaying world. We see how people are inflamed by lewd theatrical displays and gladiatorial games. Violent bands of soldiers, barbarian marauders and slave hunters roam our countryside, raping, pillaging. I fear, dear Mary, that your optimism about human nature is misplaced. Your defense of embodied sexual love and passion is hard to accept. Are not you selectively remembering the positive, optimistic words of the Gospels and forgetting the warnings and hard sayings?

**Mary:** While I must deny your last reference to selective forgetting, I agree with some of what you say. But perhaps having come to another moment of impasse, we can take a rest from our dialogue. We can continue the challenge of exploring our differences tomorrow.

## For Reflection

- *How have I tried to cultivate my abilities for sexual loving and wholehearted giving to my spouse? How have I tried to avoid being begrudging, or passive, or being intimate and passionate with my spouse?*

- *Does the vulnerability involved in opening myself to passion, intimacy and love frighten me? Why or why not?*

- *How have I tried to grow more unselfish in my loving and made efforts to integrate sexuality in a balanced way into my whole life with all of its family and work demands?*

- *In what ways am I willing to immerse myself in the beauty of creation? In the mystical beauty of my Creator?*

## Closing Prayer

Late have I loved Thee, O Beauty so ancient and so new, late have I loved Thee! You were within me, and I was in the world outside myself. I search for you outside myself and disfigured as I was, I fell upon the lovely things of your creation. You were with me, but I was not with you. The beautiful things of this world kept me far from you and yet, if they had not been in you they would have had no being at all. You called me; you cried aloud to me; you broke my barrier of deafness. You shone upon me; your radiance enveloped me; you put my blindness to flight. You shed your fragrance about me; I drew breath and now I gasp for your sweet odor. I tasted you, and now I hunger and thirst for you. You touched me, and I am inflamed with love of your peace. When at last I cling to you with all my being, for me there will be no more sorrow, no more toil. Then at last I shall be alive with true life, for my life will be wholly filled by you.[3]

## Notes

[1] Sebastian Moore, *Jesus, the Liberator of Desire* (New York: Crossroad, 1989), p. 104.

[2] *Confessions*, Book VIII, 11, p. 176.

[3] *Confessions*, Book X, 27-28, p. 231.

# Day Three
## A Friendship of Equals

### Coming Together in the Spirit

A heroine in a recent novel expresses pain at being ignored by her lover after a disagreement. This brilliant young woman is a thoroughly modern female: She is searching for love while pursuing a career as an anthropologist. As she mulls over her complaint she thinks, "I deserved to be talked to about yesterday. If my intervention was stupid I deserved to be comforted. I needed to be kept from succumbing to a certain metaphor for marriage I was recurring to too often, that is, of marriage as a form of slowed-down wrestling where the two parties keep trying different holds on each other until one of them gets tired and goes limp, at which point you have the canonical happy marriage, voila."[1]

Obviously this feisty heroine is not about to go limp, no matter how much in love she finds herself. She neither wants to dominate or be dominated. Instead she desires an exemplary marriage characterized by justice, passion and friendship. Only in such a relationship of loving equality can she talk freely to her mate, only then can she ask to be comforted or be able to offer comfort to him. Another fine thing about equality in her mind is that this kind of relationship allows a couple to have more fun.

Our heroine believes that lovers should be

ıe means that you
ıd delight your beloved
.. As she puts it, "causing
ınate is something people
ım or getting attractive
ıeeping permanent intimate
ınt than any other one

ıo play well together both
partn\..                          to abide by the same rules.
Neither the ma\.               oman can be so defensive or
take themselves so seriously that they always have to win.
This ideal condition may be difficult to sustain if men
always feel themselves entitled to the superior position.
Our heroine claims that her lover, Nelson Denoon, is
different from most of the men she has ever known. And
why? Because in the course of joking together he "had
early on made it clear I was free to include him and his
foibles as ingredients and props in my routine if I felt like
it."[4]

For the first time in her life this strong young woman
finds herself "dealing with an actual mature male, a
concept which up until then I had considered an
essentially literary construct. I was surprised at how
pleased I felt to get such deep, easy thorough laughter out
of him."[5] And as might be expected with a truly mature
male, he expends an equal amount of effort to be
delightful company for her.

Moral: In just, passionate and equal marital
friendships laughter, wit and humor add to the mutual
pleasures enjoyed and strengthen the bond of unity. Every
good thing shared in marriage—laughter, sex, babies,
work—is more than doubled. A mature man and woman
can "run their course with joy" like the sun in the heaven;
they may make "a joyful noise to the Lord."

## Defining Our Thematic Context

In a good loving marriage justice must reign. "Justice is love's absolute minimum,"[6] as Pope Paul VI wisely proclaimed. A marriage built on a proper foundation of equal dignity and respect becomes an intimate marital friendship that can flourish.

## Opening Prayer

Lord, let us grow in faithful friendship with those we love. May justice and kindness meet as we abide by your truth in every word and deed. No matter how we are tempted keep us from betraying a trust. Help married men and women become steadfast friends who open their hearts to one another. Dearest God, you are the source of life, love and joy, help us to laugh and play as our youth is renewed in your Spirit.

# RETREAT SESSION THREE

**Mary:** Come, my friend, let us celebrate the goods of marriage. I agree with your teaching that these include the faithfulness of the spouses to one another, the permanence of their commitment and bond, and the procreation of children. Such goods bring happiness to those who are married, engender holiness and benefit the common good.

**Augustine:** Yes, I have written much in favor of marriage. We Christians, unlike the pagans, believed that divorce was forbidden. Women in particular could not be put away and divorced because of infertility. Then following the Lord we demanded that both men and women should live up to the same moral standards of faithfulness in marriage. Believe me, this went against the wisdom of the Roman world and caused us no end of trouble. But I can only be thankful for this good news of our gracious Lord. As I have written to echo fervently Paul's teaching, we should thank God for creating male and female so that "in your spiritual grace they are as one. Your grace no more discriminates between them according to their sex than it draws distinction between Jew and Greek or slave and freemen."[7]

Christians also must scandalize the wisdom of the world when they insist that rich and poor are equal in the Kingdom of God. To use marriage and strategic divorce as the pagans did in order to further a family's fortune or ensure political alliances is not a Christian practice. Admittedly, these pagan practices were so approved and entrenched in the customs of my world that even I was betrothed by my mother to a Catholic heiress, partly to gain a fortune and influence to serve my career in the world, and partly to produce legitimate grandchildren. Well, of course I ended up renouncing marriage along with my worldly ambitions.

**Mary:** Yet you preached on equality in marriage in a way that helped Christians grow beyond their former limitations.

**Augustine:** Yes, preaching the gospel truth of the equal moral demand upon men and women in Christian marriage deeply offended the men of my unruly congregations. As you can imagine, men in their pride and lust to dominate did not relish having their sexual freedom constrained, or their moral superiority questioned.

Alas, it has been my humbling experience to find that women are far superior to men in their ability to practice the Christian virtues of chastity and fidelity in marriage. My longtime mistress, with whom I had a son, remained chaste after she returned to Africa. Yet I was so enslaved to lust that I took a temporary mistress so that I need not abstain for the two years which had to pass before my wealthy fiancee was old enough to marry. My first mistress was strong in her continence "but I was too unhappy and weak to imitate this example set me by a woman."[8]

Of course, when it came to women's virtue I also had the wonderful example of my mother. Monica was always stronger, more devout and charitable in her daily life than my father, Patricius. He, although "the soul of kindness," was hot-tempered, unfaithful to her and resistant to Christianity until he lay upon his deathbed. Monica was from her youth a devout Christian woman and scrupulously faithful to her marriage vows. As I say, "She had the weak body of a woman but the strong faith of a man."[9] Although, on second thought, considering what I know and have just said about the weakness of most men, perhaps I should describe her as having the strong faith of a highly devout and holy man.

**Mary:** Here again I note with sorrow that you usually refer to women as weak and constantly hark back to the belief that Eve was the instigator of the fall of Adam which brought death into the world. That theory reveals the misogyny, or hate for women, which prejudices so many religious authors in our Hebrew Scriptures and affected so many of the writers of your time. Believe me this not what our Lord taught us; he was born of woman and spoke of Wisdom and all of her children. At least you have the grace to see that in the Kingdom and new creation women are equal in grace and should not be despised among Christians—just as you have the honesty to admit it when you find women actually more faithful than their male counterparts.

I wonder. Perhaps women are more faithful in marriage because of some innate differing sexual predisposition between men and women, or as seems just as likely, because most women are raised and trained from childhood to become nurturing wives and mothers. You speak of your mother's girlhood and her upbringing in a virtuous Christian family but say nothing of your father's family background. Surely you would agree that many men are raised with a great sense of self-focused entitlement; they are taught to domineer and exert their will over others in order to prove their manliness. In a violent, sexually libertine and aggressive society men are encouraged by their peers to indulge in sexual pleasures and to pursue power, money and worldly success. This appears to be the case in your Roman world.

**Augustine:** Yes, I deeply regret those sins of my youth when I went along with the crowd in order to be accepted and gain popularity. How perverse it was that sometimes as a student in Carthage I would feel ashamed that I would not join in the cruel sports and jokes of the wildest "wreakers," who led the pack of rowdies among us. To be ashamed of being virtuous is truly perverse—a mark of the disintegration of the inner self in fallen humanity.

It is painful to confess that during my youth I often rebelled against God and all that is good, simply in order to do evil for its own sake. To do the forbidden thing was the main object of my behavior. Stealing pears, gratifying my lust in church, giving in to the wanton pleasures and excitements of Carthage—these were essentially acts of self-willed rebellion arising from my pride.

But to return to the dispute over the nature of men versus women, are you implying that women in another time and place who are raised differently might have as much difficulty as men in remaining faithful to their marriage vows? Perhaps you are right. I did have to correct my adversary Julian of Eclanum when he made the ridiculous claim that women do not experience sexual desire, or know concupiscence. While Cato, the great Roman, says that sexual desire in women is particularly disgusting, I hold that after the fall, no one, neither male nor female, can be exempt from this infection of rebellious sexuality.

My reply to Julian was apt, I think. I said that in the case of assessing female lust we might "ask Joseph how intensely women can be affected by its onslaught."[10] You remember how in the scriptural story, Joseph had to suffer when Potiphar's wife falsely accused him of rape after he chastely refused her lustful importunings (see Genesis 39:6-20).

I conclude that no matter who has been infected more by the disease of concupiscence, all men and women can only be healed of their lust by Christ. All must have their desires transformed by grace in order to be faithful and true. The marriage bond ensures that the two become one, as our Lord preached, and this permanent unity and faithful commitment is one of the greatest goods of marriage.

Over the years I watched my mother Monica patiently bear my father's infidelities, even though he loved and respected her. Eventually she won him over to Christianity, but it was a long struggle. Monica was unusual among the wives of her day because of her tact and patience; she also was unlike the other wives we knew because she was never beaten by her husband and never had to appear in public marked by wounds. Monica constantly counseled the wives of her acquaintance and told them that they should be more like herself; they should reread their marriage contracts wherein they promised to obey their masters and learn to guard their tongues while serving their husbands more willingly.

**Mary:** Now you stir me up, indeed. When you write of these episodes in Monica's married life I am amazed that you never voice any repugnance at the fact that most of the men you knew regularly beat their wives, leaving obvious marks of their assaults. Your silence at these offenses is all the more strange since you write so passionately of how much you hated being beaten as a schoolboy. As you suffered so much fear and sorrow in school you make a good case for how counterproductive beating is for any kind of love of learning or growth in wisdom to develop. So why do you not protest wife-beating as an equally horrible practice, that offends against charity?

Worse yet, you give the impression that these other wives deserved their beatings, since they, unlike Monica, would not follow her advice and become as docile and silently subservient as she was.

**Augustine:** I see your point. I don't think I've ever connected the pain and sorrow of my floggings at school, and my general pity for schoolboys, with pity for the habitual practice of beating wives and slaves. Perhaps I became numbed in this regard because cruelty and brutality were so common in my Roman society.

All of this suffering in the world, even in Christian marriages, is one of the reasons I recommended the life of virginity in dedicated communities as the better way for Christians to live. Our women who dedicate themselves to virginity are not exploited and Christian men do not sin so easily when they are kept away from temptation. (I never allowed women to set foot in the monastic community I established in my household as a bishop.)

I say this partly because all of my preaching against abuses of power, riches and sexuality in and out of marriage seem to have had such little effect. Yet, in the matter of marriage, despite my own preferences, I have always, like Saint Paul, taught that the husband must love his wife as his own flesh and sacrifice himself for her. Each spouse has authority over the other's body equally. I have always tried to defend the goodness of marriage and the dignity of Christian women. I teach the good news that women, whether married or dedicated virgins, can be great friends of God, glorious martyrs and saintly exemplars to all the Christian community. And of course I include you, Mary, as one of the greatest examples of sainthood that have glorified our Church.

I recognize, too, that women influence every child that comes into the world. In my writing of my own story I say how I wondered upon life in the womb for "I have myself seen women who are pregnant."[11] I have learned much about myself and others from watching infants and babies. As I say, I know that God allows us "to learn much from what women have to tell."[12]

**Mary:** Yes, dear Augustine, I do respond to that part of your nature which appreciates and responds to women. You extol not only the holy virgin martyrs like Thecla, but the courage of the holy married martyrs like Crispina and Perpetua. You mention the bravery of Crispina in her martyrdom to show that chaste married women also can rise to holiness. While you always exalt virginity as higher than marriage, you do make the point that either way of life can be lived well—or badly. If dedicated virgins indulge in drunkenness you make no bones about condemning them. And you criticize the vanity of those dedicated virgins who take pains to show off their elaborate little braids beneath their fine and luxurious veils. So, I notice, you never stopped observing the ways of women!

Your courteous letters to eminent women implicitly treat them as equals in learning. And who would not be edified to see that you once wrote to encourage a studious young girl to continue her studies? How good that you, a great bishop and famous scholar, would willingly offer to help a young woman in her search for wisdom.

Perhaps you should credit your awareness of women to the love you felt for your nurses who, you say, fondled you, played and laughed with you as a baby. And then there is your great love and appreciation of your mother. I also admire that you once told your mother that she was welcome to join in your conversations which were going to be distributed as classical dialogues. She was hesitant, but you assured her that women have done philosophy and that you liked her philosophy.

And while you do not allude to it directly, surely the intense love you had for your first mistress must also have made you more sensitive to women. After all, when you say that one of the things that held you back from your Christian conversion was that "I thought it would be too much for me to bear if I were to be deprived of woman's love,"[13] you give testimony to feminine influences on you. Of course you describe this feeling as a "weakness." But why, dear friend? Why do you so often interpret love as lust and see loving dependence on a beloved as an unfortunate form of attachment to the world? Indeed I would see what you call your weakness as a sign of your loving nature and your appreciation for the loving women in your past.

Few people have noted, and certainly not your

enemies and detractors, that even as a boy you chose to recite the women's parts in the Latin classics you studied at school. How I wish I could have seen you weeping over the tale of Dido dying for love of Aeneas! Or earning your prize for declaiming scorned Juno's speech! You say you used "to recite verses about Medea's flight through the air,"[14] but did not believe them. Maybe not, but attending to Medea's sad betrayal and abandonment by her spouse along with all the other tales of women's sorrow may have influenced you.

You dismiss all these youthful experiences as so much false trumpery of the pagan world and say that when you first went to Carthage to study you "cared nothing but to love and be loved."[15] You say this to berate yourself; but don't we all desire to love and be loved? Isn't love, after all, what the Christian life and marriage is all about?

**Augustine:** Yes, but in my case I could not distinguish "the clear light of true love from the murk of lust."[16] I was not aiming for a good marriage. Unfortunately, my parents had not arranged a marriage for me in my youth because they were ambitious for my worldly advancement. If my studies were going to pave the way for a great career then I could not become entangled in a mediocre marriage tying me to my small backwater town. Consequently, I am sorry to say that in Carthage I sank into fornication and "a whirlpool of sin."[17]

Then when I fell in love and my love was returned, "in the midst of my joy I was caught up in the coils of trouble, for I was lashed with the cruel, fiery rods of jealousy and suspicion, fear, anger, and quarrels."[18] Perhaps it was these turbulent experiences, aided as you would have it by my sympathy for betrayed women in poetry, which led me to understand that one of the chief goods of marriage is mutual faithfulness. Only the goods of Christian marriage can remedy the evils accompanying the disorder of sexual desires. To preserve order the mind must rule and govern the body just as the husband must rule in the household and the wife must obey.

Of course I hasten to add that those whose role it is to govern and rule must rule through sacrificial love and example, whether in the home or in the monastery.

**Mary:** Obedience, obedience, order and hierarchy—these are your constant messages, aimed especially at women. Ah, this idea of wifely obedience has caused much oppression in the family and abuses of power. You say that the obedience of wives is enjoined by Paul and necessary for good order in marriage. But don't you forget that Paul also admonishes the spouses to obey one another? Worse still, when you say that women should be governed by men the way the body should be governed by the mind you categorize women as having a nature that you deem radically different from men, that is, lower, inferior. If, however, Christians must hold that women are like the body and men are like the head of a person, then women will always be oppressed and subjected to abuses of power.

**Augustine:** But, my dear lady, in Church and society and the family, hierarchical order must be served, or all of society along with the Church will be racked by chaos and confusion. Peace and harmonious order must be kept in the domestic sphere as well as in the larger society. Indeed the whole creation is constituted of glorious hierarchies through which we ascend to God—from the flesh, to the mind, to the spiritual mysteries.

**Mary:** How you keep praising those neo-Platonic philosophers with their talk of ascending hierarchies toward eternal immutability. All your writing has been so influenced by Plotinus, whom you credit as the philosopher who finally helped you to understand that God is not a material concrete entity. Since this epiphany allowed you to finally become a Christian I suppose we should be grateful. Yet, to my mind, you seem to keep falling back into your own simplistic notion of the flesh, much as you write against a too-concrete misunderstanding of how this term was used by Saint Paul. Despite your protests that evil is only perversion of the will and an absence of good, evil for you often tends to be identified with human embodiment and with sexual desires. And when you do that, not only does all sex come to be seen as bad, but women who appear to be more involved in the bodily life of reproduction will be relegated into an inferior status.

**Augustine:** No, no. I protest. I constantly say that the term flesh cannot be seen as physical but as a word symbolizing a person's living by the self's standards rather than by God's goodness and truth. I maintain that evil and sin can only arise from voluntary perversions of the will and never from the body. But I do hold that since sexuality always arises against the will it must be seen as that part of the human person's disorder that is an apt punishment for Adam and Eve's rebellion against God. And yes, this flaw in our fallen condition does have implications for the relationship between the sexes. I sum this up quite convincingly when I say, "And just as in man's soul there are two forces, one which is dominant because it deliberates and one which obeys because it is subject to such guidance, in the same way, in the physical sense, woman has been made for man. In her mind and her rational intelligence she has a nature the equal of man's, but in sex she is physically subject to him in the same ways our natural impulses need to be subjected to the reasoning power of the mind, in order that the actions to which they lead may be inspired by the principles of good." Indeed, I am thankful to God who "made rational action subject to the rule of the intellect, as woman is subject to man."[19]

**Mary:** Augustine, Augustine. Can you not see how insulting these words are to intelligent women! Here you seem in one statement again to affirm women's equality and yet consign them to a weaker irrational condition which must be subjected to men. More worrisome, your talk of two principles within man and their constant inner warfare reminds me so much of the dualistic tenets of those Manichean heretics you supposedly left behind on your journey to Christianity. And your view of the order and authority of the father within the family sounds like you have totally conformed to the pagan Roman world you so often criticize.

When we walked with the Lord we disciples did not live by your rigid Roman ideals of hierarchies in authority. Jesus told us to always put each other first; the last shall be first and the first shall be last. He told us to become as a child, to seek to be like him and be the servant of all. I remember so well how liberating it was to be with Jesus because we women disciples were treated as equals instead of with the usual oppression. His graciousness and power were dedicated to service, love, healing and friendship. He inspired us all to try to follow him in his compassion, humility and loving ministry to a suffering world. When any of the disciples vied for first place he rebuked them and told us that relationships in God's Kingdom would be different from those existing in the world where those in authority lord it over others. Nor did gender or family relationships determine your place among his disciples. He dearly loved his mother and his family, but he also loved his disciples and the family created by following God's will. I certainly don't recognize Jesus' practice in your views of the hierarchical relationships that must be followed everywhere—and especially not within the union of marriage. Jesus called us to be his friends and insisted that we would do greater works than he.

If friendship is the model you espouse for married persons then how can there be subjection of one to another? Between friends there must be equality because only equality makes it possible to have openness of heart and mind.

**Augustine:** Surely no one who has ever known me could think that I do not understand friendship.

**Mary:** Yes, I know. When you talk about how friends love each other and delight in each other's company and do small favors for one another and encourage and support each other even through disagreements, you show that you understand friendship. And you never lived without your lifelong friends and relatives around you. Through your letters and correspondence you multiplied your friendships and extended them across the Mediterranean Sea. But as you say, there is no substitute for actually having your friends face-to-face with you.

What I do not hear, however, is the presence of a close woman friend who is your equal in scholarship or powers of mind. Did you never have such a woman friend? I wonder what your sister was like and why you never mention her even though she was the head of the community of holy women who lived near you in Hippo. Perhaps, if your first mistress had been more of an equal companion, equal in class and education, perhaps then you could imagine that marriage should be an equal relationship of friendship and that it can include a loving sexual bond.

**Augustine:** Yes, you are right. I have had only intimate male friends, with the exception of my mother. Could there be such a married relationship wherein I could find in a woman my other self? I found this kind of closeness in the friend of my youth who died early and I found it in my mother in another way. But could such an intimate equal friendship be possible in a wife? If one had such a wife, would not the relationship be spoiled by the presence of sexual desires? The Roman ideal has always been for an older man to marry a young girl and then tutor his wife to become his wise helpmate. Wives were to speak frankly to their husbands, and man and wife were to live in concord and friendship. But to advocate sexual passion within marriage would seem to go against both Christian and pagan ideals.

**Mary:** I do not know if you are correct in your austere view of how the ideal Roman gentleman would eschew sexual passion in his decorous marriage. Do you remember Ausonius, the pagan classical scholar who tutored the Emperor?

**Augustine:** Of course, he was a friend of my friend and mentor, the great Paulinus, a noble Christian humanist and scholar. When Ausonius the poet and humanist was tutor to the emperor it was thought auspicious. Perhaps a humanist scholar might be able to exert some influence on the military-minded Roman regime. Ausonius gained such influence in the empire that his son and son-in-law came to Carthage as prefects when I was a young teacher of rhetoric. Why do you ask?

**Mary:** Because of his poetic testimony to the existence of another kind of Roman marriage than those sober Latin authorities you cite. Ausonius married and loved his wife dearly, she was another self for him. We know this because, unlike your other models of decorum and control, he could write this poem.

Uxor, vivamusque ut viximus et teneamus
  nomina, quae primo sumpsimus in thalamo:
nec ferat ulla dies, ut commutemur in aevo,
  Quin tibi sim iuvenis tuque puella mihi.

(Let us live, dear wife, as we have always lived, still exchanging the endearments we whispered in the marriage chamber, let no passage of time change our ages at all; I will remain your young lover, you my new bride.)[20]

**Augustine:** These words bring tears to my eyes. Many painful words remain in my heart. Forgive me if I retire from our dialogue until another day.

## For Reflection

- *How have I worked for a just love and equal friendship in my marriage, so that each partner has been held morally equal and each has been able to receive what is needed to flourish?*

- *In what ways have I loved my partner faithfully and paid enough attention to his or her uniqueness? How have I expressed appreciation and gratitude for our love?*

- *How have we as a couple cultivated playfulness, joy, pleasure and good humor in our marital friendship? How have we reached out to others in their physical, psychic and spiritual needs?*

## Closing Prayer

O Lord...When we love our neighbor giving him help for his bodily needs, our souls bear fruit in works of mercy proper to their kind, for they have seed in them according to their species.... Then we are like a great tree bearing fruit, for we do good to a neighbor, if he is the victim of wrong, by rescuing him from the clutches of his assailant and providing him with the firm support of true justice, just as a tree affords the protection of its shade.

In this way, O Lord you create happiness and give it to us to ease our lives. In this same way, I pray, may faithfulness grow up out of the earth and redress look down from heaven. Let there be luminaries in the vault of the sky. Let us share our bread with the hungry, give the poor and the vagrant a welcome to our houses, meet the naked, clothe him, and from our own flesh and blood turn not away. These good deeds are the fruits that spring from the earth. Look on them and say, "It is good that this is so." Let our light shine out in the world and from this humble crop of good deeds let us pass on to that more sublime harvest, the joy of contemplation, so that we may come to possess the Word of Life and shine in the world like stars set in the firmament of your Scripture.[21]

## Notes

[1] Norman Rush, *Mating* (New York: Alfred A. Knopf, 1991), p. 381.

[2] Ibid., p. 221.

[3] Ibid.

[4] Ibid., pp. 221-222.

[5] Ibid., p. 222.

[6] Pope Paul VI, Address to the Eucharistic Congress.

[7] *Confessions*, Book XIII, 23, p. 333.

[8] Ibid., Book VI, 15, p. 131.

[9] *Confessions*, Book IX, 4, p. 186.

[10] Augustine, *Against Julian*, trans. Matthew A. Schumacher, C.S.C., in *The Fathers of the Church: A New Translation*, Vol. 35 (New York: Fathers of the Church, Inc., 1957), p. 266.

[11] *Confessions*, Book I, 6, p. 26.

[12] Ibid.

[13] Ibid., Book VI, 11, p. 128.

[14] Ibid., Book III, 6, p. 62.

[15] Ibid., Book III, 1, p. 55.

[16] Ibid., Book II, 2, p. 43.

[17] Ibid., Book III, 1, p. 55.

[18] Ibid.

[19] Ibid., Book XIII, 32, 34, p. 344, 345.

[20] Quoted in Erich Segal, "Vita, Ausonius of Bordeaux," Brief Life of an Unclassifiable Poet: ca.310-ca. 395, *Harvard Magazine*, November-December, 1995, p. 58.

[21] *Confessions*, Book XIII, 17-18, p. 324, 325.

# Day Four
## Embracing Life

### Coming Together in the Spirit

Before the eighteenth and nineteenth centuries, when more women authors entered the literary game, it is almost impossible to find a novel or a play depicting a happy marriage in which both partners are equally respected. However, in 1818 Jane Austen provides us with that endearing couple: Admiral and Mrs. Croft in *Persuasion*, her romantic comic novel turned into a popular 1995 movie. The Crofts are described as exceptional because unlike most married couples, they are "particularly attached and happy";[1] they share similar tastes, have feelings in unison and generally delight in each other's countenance and companionship. During their long marriage they have sailed the seven seas together on five different ships. When on land they continue to indulge "their country habit of always being together." On visits to Bath they walk about "in happy independence," or contentedly sit at home reading by their fireside, or they jointly socialize with fellow naval officers "with Mrs. Croft looking as intelligent and keen as any of the officers around her." Sophia Croft repeatedly declares that women are "rational creatures" and so can be quite comfortable and safe aboard ship with their sailor husbands. After all, "while we were together, you know, there was nothing to be feared"; besides, "none of us expect to be in smooth water all our days."

In the Crofts' happy and equal marital partnership, all decisions are made conjointly. Even when careering about the countryside in their brand new horse and gig, Mrs. Croft not only gives warnings of danger—"My dear Admiral, that post; we shall certainly take that post"—but often sees them safely home by "coolly giving the reins a better direction herself." Then they neither fall into a rut, run afoul of a dung-cart, nor overturn. The Crofts' style of cooperative driving was "no bad representation of the general guidance of their affairs." So here's one recipe for a good marriage: Whether on land or sea, in rough or smooth water, keep a loving unity of heart and mind— and let the reins be shared.

## Defining Our Thematic Context

To achieve marital happiness one must grow up and become an adult in an intimate partnership with another. The marital journey is always in progress, but it may take a decade or so to fully develop a deep and compatible union which is irreversible. Christians who aspire to grow up into Christ will be seeking to love one other as God loves us.

Christ's friendship with us gives us a trustworthy pattern for the fast friendship of marriage. A couple's efforts to increase in courteous lovingkindness will be rewarded; they will be fruitful and have their youth renewed like the eagle's. As "the Lord takes pleasure in his people," and the faithful exult and "sing for joy on their couches," so a longmarried couple can become merry and wise.

## Opening Prayer

Lord, may our marriages become increasingly fruitful in every way. In differences between friends let us find the way to Christ, our Truth. You know that we need you to become transformed in heart and mind. If children are born to us let us rejoice in our love and care for them. When those we love suffer and die let us trust in your gracious mercy and lovingkindness.

# RETREAT SESSION FOUR

**Augustine:** Dear lady, I have been moved by our dialogue and have reflected upon what you say. Now in order not to be misunderstood by you or our retreatants I must clarify several points I have made in my writings on marriage. While I am sure that God's existence ensures that an eternally true justice and morality exist always and everywhere, I also have recognized that "offenses against human codes of conduct vary according to differences of custom."[2] History is the record of how peoples have lived in the past in different places. I point out that marriage for the patriarchs and founders of Israel was different than it is in our times. In what I call, "the mysterious difference of times,"[3] the patriarchs were allowed to have more wives and even concubines "for the sake of copious posterity," a practice which certainly is not lawful now for us as Christians.

But now you stimulate me to think about the differences of times in a new way. Perhaps we could ask ourselves whether marriage might not change in the future as well as it has in the past? You claim that my defense of women's equality of nature in the Lord must result in an equality of authority within the marital relationship and in the family. And knowing you, you probably envision equality for women in civil society and before the law!

Your ideas of women and marriage seem farfetched to me, but at least I have confessed that "I am not ignorant of the fact that the question of marriage still remains very obscure and involved. Nor dare I say that either in this work or in any other up to the present have I explained all its intricacies...."[4]

**Mary:** Your modesty and your ability to enter into dialogue with your own past positions reveals the Augustine I admire as the great intellectual who always ardently seeks God's truth wherever it may be found. I honor the fact that in your final days you reread all your works in order to add things or make changes that you thought necessary. And always you display such sensibility as well as a good measure of common sense.

**Augustine:** And you Mary are much too generous in your praises. However, it is true that I believe in good sense and in taking the world and God's created reality seriously as it really exists for us. As I say, "Just because our Lord, when he wished suddenly turned water into wine is no excuse for us not to understand the proper value of water as water."[5]

**Mary:** Yes, I love this point of yours, and also cannot resist reminding you that the water turned into wine was a miracle performed to increase the level of celebration and intoxicated joy at a marriage feast. And it was done at the behest of a woman, my dear friend and mentor, Mary, the Lord's great mother, aptly called the first disciple.

Strong mothers produce strong sons, a case well proved by Monica and yourself. But just as Monica did, I, too, can criticize you as well as sing your praises. Do you, in fact, always understand the proper value of water as water? Do you truly appreciate the ordinary goodness of marriage as marriage, or the body as the body, or women as women?

**Augustine:** Enough, enough. I grant you that to understand the proper value of anything is no easy task. I humbly admit that understanding the mystery of our faith, understanding how we are embodied and how all bodies are interconnected in the Church is a truth so deep and complex that "I cannot comprehend it."[6]

**Mary:** Yes, Christians do well to engage in dialogues and vigorous open discussions so that we can make sense of the Good News. The church always must seek to understand more fully God as Truth and Wisdom—even though it leads to conflicts and debates. Certainly, creative conflict between friends and among the married can be used to further mutual understanding and growth in wisdom. So I agree with you when, in your prime, you commend Paul's words to the Corinthians that disagreement between different parties in the Church is necessary to arrive at authentic truth. So, my dear friend, I choose to dialogue with Augustine, the perpetual seeker of truth, who is open to disagreement and arguments.

**Augustine:** My strong mother certainly never hesitated to oppose me; she was relentless and always terribly sure of her position. She was more open to correction from our admired mentor, the great Ambrose, than she ever was from me. At the end of her life she told me I had always been a wonderful son to her. But in my period as a heretic and unbeliever she never, ever conceded in an argument that she was wrong and that I might be right. At one point in our struggles over religion she even barred me from her household.

**Mary:** Yes, and I know you admired her faith and unbending resolve. But sometimes a strong unyielding faith can be blind, or even obdurate because of narrowness and a lack of learning. I think your approach to seeking truth through engagement with everyone and everything in creation is a better way to wisdom.

On this note, let me ask you about something else that puzzles me in your views. We have already argued over your contradictory view that women are in Christ equal in nature, equally capable of being morally responsible in marriage, and yet at the same time deemed by you to be the weaker and inferior sex. I see other contradictions in your views regarding reproduction and the value of having children.

**Augustine:** Are you referring to my admission that I only begrudgingly accepted the birth of my son Adeodatus? But I explain my reluctance. It arose from the fact that my mistress and I were living together only to satisfy our passions and were not united in a Christian marriage. We were not trying to have children or build up a Christian family—far from it. But please give me credit. Remember that I also say that "when babies come we cannot help but love them."[7] I did love Adeodatus whose very name means a gift of God. When he grew up he was a wonderfully intelligent Christian youth full of gifts and graces; I took great pride in him and included his words in the dialogues I was composing at that period of my life.

**Mary:** Yes, your love and pride in your son show clearly.

But this appreciation and love for him makes it even more disturbing to me that you can later aver that because of original sin every infant in the womb is tainted and doomed to damnation. You depict infants coming into the world crying for sorrow and bewailing their fallen nature. According to your pessimistic message even some baptized infants may not be adopted into eternal life. If this negative view of reproduction is true, how can you continue to maintain that one of the goods of marriage is the procreation of children? Is it a good thing for the married to produce children who may be destined for eternal perdition?

Surely you are wrong about this. It is hardly in accord with our Hebrew Scriptures' understanding that children are one of the chief blessings of life. While, unfortunately, a quiverful of sons was more favored than the birth of daughters, still offspring are valued as a wonderful reward for fulfilling God's command to increase and multiply.

**Augustine:** Well first of all, I hold that in the new creation humankind does not *have* to procreate and increase according to the flesh; only the patriarchs of Israel had to have children in order to ensure the survival of the people. Since Christ's conquest of death we no longer need physical procreation to fight back against dying. Celibacy and continence in the Kingdom serve as signs that the Kingdom has come and reverse the reign of death which necessitated procreation. Now we can produce spiritual children and possess eternal life through baptism into the faith; every Christian can become a fruitful member of Christ's family through acts of faith.

**Mary:** I agree that we are not required to have children to be saved or to validate our lives, and, yes, we do belong to a family in Christ's company of beloved brothers and sisters in the Lord. Indeed, women are liberated by our Christian teaching because our value as whole persons no longer depends upon our producing children, or on our being sexually pleasing to men, or upon making good marital alliances to benefit the power and wealth of the biological family.

**Augustine:** And as for the command in Genesis to increase and multiply, I think that this now should be interpreted symbolically. In my commentary on Genesis in my *Confessions* I explain this command by writing, "I take the reproduction of human kind to refer to the thoughts which our minds conceive, because reason is fertile and productive. I am convinced that this is what was meant, O Lord, when you commanded man and the creatures of the sea to increase and multiply."[8]

**Mary:** Increase and multiply our thoughts? How ridiculous! If not downright heretical! I take back my earlier comment that you always display common sense. Now you are proving that the most brilliant people, the best and the brightest, can be led astray in service of some pet theory or bias. In your anti-sexual prejudices you are denigrating God's creation by denying the goods of embodied procreation, not to mention repudiating Jesus' own teachings and example. Our Lord confirmed in word and deed his approval of marriage, as well as pointing out how good it is to have children that you love and care for; he uses our human love for our children as a way for us to understand God's love for us.

And how you overestimate the importance of abstract reasoning! I'm surprised you don't praise Athena's birth from Zeus' forehead, from whence as the myth informs us, she burst forth full grown and armored. That kind of asexual rational reproduction would have the added advantage for you of doing away with sex, women, babies and original sin all in one fell swoop.

**Augustine:** Calm yourself, dear lady. Now it is you who do not appear willing to listen, or to learn from the dialogue you extol.

You will be happy to know that when I thought more carefully on this command to increase and multiply, I came to accept the existence of procreation in paradise before the fall. I finally decided that, yes, there would have been both marriage and children born in paradise. But they would have been conceived calmly by deliberate will, not by immoderate sexual passion. And Eve would not have her body violated or experience pangs and suffering in childbirth. Childbirth, like sleep, fatigue, illness or death, would not be forced upon the human body.

When the requisite number of predestined saints that God planned for humankind had been born into paradise then there would have been an end to procreation. A calm gladness of heart and eternal life would reign without the presence of death or sexual desire.

Now, Mary, hear me out. Reflect on the problem of the existence of sin and evil in our world. Surely some enormous and grievous wound in our human nature must be at the root of so much perversion; only the prior existence of an original sin and fall provides an adequate explanation of the enormity of humankind's propensities for evil. So, logically, it must be the case that if all of humankind is united and all are fallen and damned by Adam's sin, then only those redeemed in baptism can be saved. Then Christian parents who are only saved by baptism, not by nature, must produce children who are like themselves, that is, naturally doomed until they, too, receive the grace of baptism. To be saved, babies must themselves be baptized into Christ's spiritual family, the Church.

While God does wondrously create children in the womb, these offspring cannot help but be infected with original sin because of the concupiscence accompanying their generation by sexual intercourse—just like their parents and their grandparents, all the way back to Cain and Abel. Parents can initiate the conception of children, but they cannot control what happens to them afterwards. Some infants may be predestined to die unbaptized and so be doomed. If you do not like this, then I advise you to "complain to God,"[9] and ask him why he allows people to be created whom he foreknows will be damned. Remember, he is all just, all good, all wise even if his mysterious ways are ineffable and incomprehensible.

**Mary:** I don't have to complain to God when I can complain to you about your distorted theology. First, there is your false assumption that original sin must result in a corrupting evil centered in sexual desire, sexual intercourse and sexual generation. This ill-begotten idea (you appreciate my pun I'm sure) is compounded by your pessimistic teaching that only an elite or an elect are predetermined to be saved—while another group of human beings, including poor babes, will be damned and abandoned by God for the sin of their parents.

Our God made visible in the Jesus Christ I know displays merciful love to every being created by God, and especially to anyone who is disadvantaged through any handicap, including the moral handicaps of sin and weakness. As Jesus reminds us, God does "not break the bruised reed, or smother the smouldering wick." Jesus passionately desires the happiness and salvation of all his beloved brothers and sisters created in God's image—a desire he sealed by his death. And the Jesus I saw tenderly receiving the children and babes in arms is especially loving and compassionate toward all little ones. Who are you to say that there can be anyone, especially any baby, who will not eventually be saved by Christ's love?

God may be mysterious, ineffable and transcendent beyond all human comprehension, but could God be as monstrous as you describe? Never. I take comfort in the Spirit and the inspired words of John's prophetic vision of the end of the world.

> "It is I, Jesus, who sent my angel to you with this testimony for the churches. I am the root and the descendant of David, the bright morning star."
> The Spirit and the bride say,
>     "Come."
> And let everyone who hears say,
>     "Come."
> And let everyone who is thirsty
>     come.
> Let anyone who wishes take the
>     water of life as a gift. (Revelation 22:16, 17)

**Augustine:** Yes, but the prophets, along with Christ predict that woes and disasters will come to the wicked who will be judged by God. In your quotation of John's revelation you leave out the verses describing the doom and destruction accompanying the end of the world in the coming Apocalypse. Remember the rain of consuming fire and the gnashing of teeth that John sees as the fate of the evil ones of this world. And the first part of those prophetic verses you quote so selectively proclaims that at the end, "Outside are the dogs and sorcerers and fornicators and murderers and idolaters, and everyone who loves and practices falsehood" (Revelation 22:15).

**Mary:** But, Augustine, have you ever known a baby who was a sorcerer, a fornicator, an idolater or a murderer? Could innocent babies or those who have never heard the gospel be held responsible for not worshipping God? I grant you that a person could in a free act of will deliberately refuse God's love and persist in the desire for what they recognize to be evil. "Evil be thou my good," says Lucifer in Milton's *Paradise Lost*. But my point is that sexual desire, sexual intercourse and procreation are not evil and not inevitably corrupting as you think. Babies are not born evil.

**Augustine:** Ah, but I have watched babies and seen that they do have hateful passions and jealousies; and I know that all children lie as I lied to my parents and teachers. From the very origin of my consciousness of self I passionately willed to be my own god and go my own greedy and rebellious way.

**Mary:** Yes, I grant you that no one escapes a certain woundedness in our human nature, a tendency to anxiety, distrust, self-will and selfishness, which will inevitably result in freely chosen voluntary acts of sin. All have sinned, except the Lord. But our woundedness is not the whole story of human nature. Children seek to grow and learn in their love affair with the world. Indeed, Christian married life and loving families are gracious schools of goodness where we can learn to overcome sin by loving one another. You in your *Confessions* rightfully give prayerful thanks for the good and gracious gifts of human nature that you possessed as an infant and child who sought the good and the true. As you say, our hearts are restless until they find their rest in God.

You are so moving in your own account of how long it took you to respond to God's effort to find and rescue you. This seems to me to be an accurate assessment of how people usually need time to develop and grow. Your later view of an elect who alone are saved from damnation appears to make no allowance for the lifetime it may take to find God.

If nothing else, think how hard this belief would be for Christians whose families remain unbelievers. You speak of how glad Monica was that on your conversion she could be assured that you were not going to be damned. And you give thanks that when your beloved Adeodatus died as a young man you knew he would not be lost to you forever because he died as a confessing Christian in this life. But couldn't you imagine that a merciful God can give persons a chance immediately after death to encounter the Divine Love more directly and clearly than they were able to in this life? Unfortunately, many people are ignorant or have been so abused and ill treated in their families that they become adults who are severely stunted and morally handicapped by the evils they have suffered.

Truly, it is the suffering of infants and children, especially the pains and deaths of our own children, that most make us confront the mystery of evil. Like you, every believer has been forced, along with Job, to cry out at the existence of so much suffering and evil in the world. But I could never approve of your dreadful solution— which appears to complacently accept evil and injustice and attribute them to God's mysterious will and plan for the world!

After walking with Jesus the Christ, I believe that God suffers every moment that any one of God's beloved children suffer. We go to meet a God who ends human suffering. Our God in that great day of the Lord "will wipe every tear from their eyes. Death will be no more; mourning and crying and pain will be no more....for 'See I am making all things new'" (Revelation 21:4, 5).

**Augustine:** Here again, dear lady, I see you becoming so impassioned that your judgment is clouded by excessive optimism. But have we not strayed from our theme?

**Mary:** Yes, we have. But can we help it? In this instance if we disagree over the lovingkindness of God and God's plan for the creation we will certainly disagree over the nature of human nature and the goods of marriage and family life. I believe that when Christians have children and love them they have an opportunity to understand God's maternal nature in a direct experiential way. There is such a joy in having children and seeing them increase in grace and wisdom—especially when they are grown and can become your friends and equals. How God must love us, for despite all our faults and all the sorrows of life we can love our children so passionately and feel so grateful and deeply blessed in having them.

**Augustine:** I think I did sense some of this in my love and joy in the young manhood of Adeodatus. But oh, the pain that goes with this kind of loving attachment. When my son died, just as when my mother died, I was forced to suffer such pangs of grief.

**Mary:** Yes, both fathers and mothers know no greater pain, I am sure, than the loss of a beloved child. That is why I wish that when John in his apocalyptic vision was quoting from Isaiah's prophecies he had included Isaiah's other comforting words describing God's holy mountain, "No more shall there be in it an infant that lives but a few days, or an old person who does not live out a lifetime" (Isaiah 65:20). The loss of children, and spouses and our parents and friends is so painful to all of us who love them, even when we believe we shall see them again in the Resurrection.

**Augustine:** Yes, but aren't you now giving evidence for my side of the argument over the desirability of marriage? It is the existence of so much pain and suffering from attachments that has made me hesitant about recommending marriage to Christians. You have all of the quarrels, and suspicious jealousies and heartbreaks of erotic love as well as the struggle to control sexual desire. Then if children come you will have all the anxieties and fears that accompany the struggles to care for them, support them and educate them. Loving your spouse and your children you will experience suffering in all their pains and their disappointments, defeats, absences, illnesses and death. And what of your worries over the moral and spiritual well-being of your family, their lapses, defections and sins? Suppose my mother had died before I was converted? She suffered more pains and worries in her laboring to give me a spiritual birth than in giving me physical birth.

And you women suffer the most, I think, with so much pain and dangers of ill health and death accompanying childbirth. Alas, marriage brings children into a world so sad that I have called it a very hellhole; marriage can only bring Christians an increase of sorrows. Even in a completely faithful Christian marriage, even when mutual continence avoids sexual storms, a multitude of other hardships and trials abound to disturb your peace. The married will inevitably suffer so much grief in mourning the pains of their children and in the losses of their beloved family members.

**Mary:** Now you touch upon wounds painful for me to bear. Every married woman who has lost a child, or watched her children suffer and die, has, like Mary, had her heart pierced with a sword. And as I know all too well, every woman who has been widowed also will grieve. I remember how tenderhearted Jesus was to widows; most poor widows in Galilee did face a bleak existence, especially if their sons died. Jesus was so moved by compassion for a widow that he restored the life of the widow's son and returned the young man to his mother.

When I think how many times Jesus out of compassion healed family members and restored them to their loved ones, I am strengthened in my disapproval of your views on marriage and family. I feel your counsel to avoid the sorrows of marriage and family goes against the gospel message. Avoid marriage because love brings so much sorrow in its wake? And this comes from a great Christian who is committed to loving others as we have been loved by God. Not to marry or procreate in order to avoid the birthing pains of human love! Augustine, I wonder if we shall ever come to a meeting of the minds.

**Augustine:** We shall see. Until tomorrow dear friend, when we may start afresh and perhaps have a more amiable discourse.

## For Reflection

- *In what ways have I seen marriage change from one generation to another, from my parents' marriage to my own? How have I seen my own marriage change and develop?*

- *What does having children mean to me? What assumptions about human nature have I brought to procreation and my goals in childrearing?*

- *What sorrows have I known in my family life? How does my belief in the Resurrection affect my grieving? How have I ministered to others who were broken by the sorrows of family life?*

- *In what ways have I experienced God's presence in the ebb and flow of joy and sorrow in my married life?*

## Closing Prayer

It is always the case that the greater the joy, the greater is the pain which precedes it. Why should this be, O lord my God, when you are your own eternal joy, you are Joy itself, you are always surrounded by creatures which rejoice in you? Why is it that in this part of your creation which we know there is this ebb and flow of progress and retreat, of hurt and reconciliation? Is this the rhythm of our world? Is this what you prescribed when from the heights of heaven to the depths of earth, from the first beginnings to the end of time, from the angel to the worm, from the first movement to the last, you allotted a proper place and a proper time to good things of every kind and to all your just works? How can I hope to understand the height and the depth of you, from the greatest to the most lowly of your works? You never depart from us, yet it is hard for us to return to you.

Come, O Lord, and stir our hearts. Call us back to yourself. Kindle your fire in us and carry us away. Let us scent your fragrance and taste your sweetness. Let us love you and hasten to your side.[10]

# Notes

1 All quotations from *Persuasion* are taken from the Little, Brown & Co. edition of 1906.

2 *Confessions*, Book III, 8, p. 65.

3 Augustine, *The Good of Marriage*, trans. Charles T. Wilcox, M.M., in *The Fathers of the Church: A New Translation*, Vol. 27 (New York: The Fathers of the Church, Inc., 1955), p. 31.

4 Augustine, *Adulterous Marriages*, trans. Charles T. Huegelmeyer, M.M., in *The Fathers of the Church: A New Translation*, Vol. 27 (New York: The Fathers of the Church, Inc., 1955), p. 98.

5 Augustine, *The Care to Be Taken for the Dead*, trans. John A. Lacey, M.A., in *The Fathers of the Church: A New Translation*, Vol. 27 (New York: The Fathers of the Church, Inc., 1955), p. 378.

6 Ibid., pp. 378, 379.

7 *Confessions*, Book IV, 2, p. 72.

8 Ibid., Book XIII, 24, p. 336.

9 *Against Julian*, p. 129.

10 *Confessions*, Book VIII, 3-4, pp. 162-163.

# DAY FIVE
## Growing Together in Marriage

### Coming Together in the Spirit

A tense and angry couple glower at each other in a *New Yorker* cartoon. The steely-eyed wife has just spoken and the caption reads, "Let's stop this before we both say a lot of things we mean."

We laugh at the unexpected twist given to a common phrase, but this ironic thrust of wit also uncovers some home truths about modern marriage. Some people will chuckle because they recognize these kinds of families, including perhaps their own, where no one reveals their true feelings about anything. In these households to "say a lot of things that you really mean" would threaten the fragile peace that is warily and wearily maintained.

Other married folk will laugh because they have endured too many sessions of emotional show-and-tell. Such encounters can clear the air but take a toll in emotional energy. Is there no happy medium in marital disclosure, or telling it like it is, or was, or might be? If you want to grow together in love and Christian charity, how do you handle the marital ebb and flow of positive and negative attitudes?

A first step consists in honestly recognizing that surges of positive and negative emotional responses will always exist between married people, as in every human encounter. Love and hate can be closely related because both are passionate, highly aroused emotions. Calm indifference is the opposite of love or hate. Alas, you can flare up and momentarily hate someone you dearly love. Once you face this shocking truth, you understand why most murders are committed within the family—and why divorces become so bitter.

Another problem in marriage is that in the ever-changing stream of rushing human consciousness a change can take place instantly. It becomes difficult to tell a permanently-changed current of feeling from a momentary eddy or irrelevant ripple. Unfortunately, people who have been too long immersed in a culture of pop psychology make mistakes when sounding the marital waters.

I once met a slow-talking Southern minister who recounted his problems in therapeutic growth groups. "They keep pushing and pushing me to say how I feel, to get in touch with my emotions and express my inner self. But I honestly have to reply that by the time my Alabama drawl trickles forth in words, I no longer feel like I did when I started the sentence." Touché. I took great pleasure in assuring my beleaguered friend that even fast-talking types couldn't keep up with the lightning speed of changes taking place in consciousness. Indeed, verbalizing an emotion changes the emotion in subtle or not-so-subtle ways; it may augment, deflate, crystallize or defuse the original feeling. Fashionable pressures to "share," or to "acknowledge your feelings," or to "get in touch with your self," may not recognize the complexities involved. Moral: It's not easy to know one's self very well, and therefore doubly hard to assess accurately one's complex relationships with a spouse. Communication is not always an all-purpose solvent to any and all personal problems.

Yet it's still necessary in a good marriage for heart to

speak to heart. There are a multitude of nonverbal ways to do this, but in our highly verbal culture you have to have face-to-face conversations to keep fully connected. Notes left on the refrigerator or messages in the answering machine will not do the job. Just as our relationship and friendship with God cannot flourish without sustained and frequent prayer and worship, neither can our marriages stay alive without openness and intimacy.

How else can we become transformed in Christ and increase in mutual charity unless we make efforts to listen?

## Defining Our Thematic Context

Conflict between married partners, like all encounters conducted by Christ's disciples, should be conducted with charity, spirited openness and nonviolent means that do no harm. As the Psalms tell us, kindness and truth must meet, justice and peace shall kiss.

Every thought and every emotion that needs to be expressed can be brought into the eternal conversation of a Christian marriage, but no attacks or wounding assaults can be countenanced. Christ's words about the danger of damnation for those who call another person a fool must be remembered. His teaching clearly outlaws the rudeness, contempt and nastiness that can mar marital conflict. Those who perfect the ability to honestly and lovingly talk to one another with Christian civility and governance of the tongue will in all likelihood remain well married.

## Opening Prayer

Lord, as we struggle to grow up in your love and love of neighbor we encounter pain that you alone can turn to benefit. Let us become willing to admonish one another in honest charity. May the marriages and families that we create be filled with your Spirit. Receive our offerings of intense happiness and bitter sorrow. Help our hearts to heal and grow whole.

# Retreat Session Five

**Augustine:** Dear lady, as we continue to disagree so "spiritedly," you are right to remember that I quote Saint Paul and also believe that conflict and discussion lead to more authentic truths and more reliable unity. I only wonder whether this kind of challenging talk could be good for a marriage.

**Mary:** Yes, I think so, because in a married friendship every facet of the self intersects with the other and the two different persons must learn to live together in harmony. I think this integration of two different and separate selves in a cooperative unity is what the Lord means when he speaks of the married couple becoming one flesh. I don't think he meant some kind of undifferentiated lump in which individual identities are lost. I always find that those who love God become more like Christ in a family resemblance, but at the same time also grow to be more distinctly themselves. The same process works for the partners in a good marriage. As two fully differentiated persons, the married couple share, cooperate and integrate their sexuality, work, play, worship, study, social life, reproductive decisions, childrearing—and everything else. They become more fully themselves, even though it has been said that the long-married begin to look alike!

The theory has it that we unconsciously and silently imitate the facial expressions of those we live with.

**Augustine:** Yes, I have observed from watching babies and other persons including myself that "there is a kind of universal language, consisting of expressions of the face and eyes, gestures and tones of voice, which can show whether a person means to ask for something and get it, or refuse it and have nothing to do with it."[1]

**Mary:** This universal language of gesture and emotion plays such an important part in marriage and sexual communication. So much is conveyed through touch, and tone and voice and gesture in the intimacy of marital life. Words are always embedded in the larger context of the give and take of emotions. You, dear Augustine, are so psychologically acute when you note how emotions increase in strength of feelings when they are expressed. This ability to intensify emotions, can work in both positive actions expressing love and adoration as well as acts of coldness and meanness.

**Augustine:** I hold that the character of the human will determines the worth of emotions. "If the will is wrongly directed the emotions will be wrong; if the will is right, the emotions will be not only blameless, but praiseworthy."[2] So both positive and negative emotions can be either good or bad. I give as an example the feelings of Saint Paul who as "Christ's athlete" expressed a whole range of emotions—jealousy, sorrow, affection, righteous indignation—in his ministry. Paul understood the centrality and the richness of Christian love.

**Mary:** This range of emotions called forth in love is why marriage can be a way to holiness. You have to share life in such close quarters, and in the midst of so many petty irritations! Every personal flaw is revealed and every virtue tested. Yet you can also have such surges of affection and joyful comfort from your spouse. Think of all the goods that your own friendships brought you and then you can imagine that the intimate lifelong support and friendship of a spouse might well give you.

**Augustine:** Yes, friendship, concord and mutual love are the essence of Christian marriage. But I must confess that when I thought about marrying and wrote soliloquies upon the subject, I could only reflect that a wife to me would have meant sensual pleasure, enough money from her dowry to support a life of leisured study and respectable children to carry on my family name. These are such worldly goods that I felt I must give them up if I was going to be a truly committed Christian. My mother in her great faith said that my Christian conversion and dedicated celibacy as a servant of God amply compensated her for the loss of grandchildren in the flesh.

**Mary:** Dedicated virginity is a blessing for the Church—although to consider it as an intrinsically superior Christian vocation seems misguided. If the Christian life were really a question of who could have the most completely attentive and undistracted focus upon God, why not follow the example of a saint like Simon Stylites who lived immobilized upon the top of a pillar and stared fixedly at heaven for twenty plus years? He was rarely distracted for a waking minute from directing his attention upon God.

**Augustine:** I take your point. My own life was filled with friends and family. But I also always found that my attachments to my friends and family made the pain of parting from them that much more intense. My grief from the loss of these people was so disturbing to my peace.

**Mary:** But, my dear Augustine, how could an increase in love not be worth the corresponding sorrows of loss? Christ came to give us life in abundance, and an abundant life will include both love and passionate attachments as well as conflicts, sorrows and grief. As you well know, since you speak of Saint Paul's range of intense feelings and describe the reality of Jesus' emotions. Besides, it is the closeness of your loving friends that let them understand you and so help you to grow in the Lord.

**Augustine:** Yes, I have always known that when you love you are granted more understanding of what you love. Perhaps the burning desire to understand focuses your attention. I recognize that a loving friend can help you to overcome your faults and appreciate your strengths.

But it is also the case that sometimes a word spoken in anger by someone who is not friendly can help you to correct your fault. When my mother Monica was young she was once quarreling with a servant who called her a drunkard for sipping drinks from her family's wine stores on the sly. And my mother took it so much to heart that she never drank too much again for the rest of her life. Also my great friend Alypius once was rebuked and shamed as a young man when he came to one of my classes in Carthage and overheard my scornful ridicule of students who wasted their time going to the games at the amphitheater. Alypius, who indulged in these pastimes, was so stung that he consequently reformed his life. So not only soft words or the comments of friends can help us to grow into Christ's maturity.

**Mary:** Yes, true, but you also agree, I am sure, that the people closest to us whom we love and admire the most can hurt us most, and so admonish us most effectively. Sometimes our dearest friends and beloved spouses can become our dearest enemies when it comes to correction. A wonderful poet from that faraway isle of Britain shares this insight when he sings of God, "Wert thou my enemy, O thou my friend, How wouldst thou worse, I wonder, than thou dost, Defeat, thwart me?"[3] Such a lament can strike home to the married, since beloved spouses, not to mention one's children, can provide us so much frustration. Families teach us so much about our selves that we might not care to know. Those who have been long married and raised children understand this paradox.

**Augustine:** Surely no Christian could deny that in our common pilgrimage to holiness we must be corrected by God and man. As you well know, I certainly defend discipline in the home, the school, the Church and the state—even at times of coercion. It seems clear to me that charity for one another means that we must instruct and admonish as well as comfort one another. I have said that we must hate the evil and the sin that another does but love the sinner. We have been told to admonish as well as bear one another's burdens; we must attend to our neighbor's physical and spiritual needs.

**Mary:** Surely married people engage in all of these Christian works of mercy at home when they feed, shelter and minister to each other's needs along with those of their children, families and people outside the family who receive their alms and hospitality. So many families give shelter, help and comfort to their needy friends and relatives. And of course, parents give constant care, support, admonition and instruction to their children.

Married partners, serving as beloved friends and enemies, admonish and correct each other's faults. They really can't help it. Partly there is the desire to see the person you love so dearly become as developed and good as they can be, and partly there is the crucial need to foster a reliable source of support from one's partner.

**Augustine:** Whether married or not, I consider it a spiritual kindness to admonish, instruct and encourage our brothers and sisters in the Lord, even when it takes effort and leads to conflict. My role as a shepherd, teacher and combatant against heretics involved me in a great deal of correction and admonition. It takes courage to say the unpleasant thing that someone would rather not hear— especially if the one to be corrected is a worldly and rich person with a great deal of power. Some of my encounters with the rich magnates of Africa and with the Roman authorities were quite unpleasant.

**Mary:** Ah, but afterwards you could always withdraw and go back to your monastic community, where you ruled and held authority. Did you have persons who lived with you who would dare to correct you? There is no hiding place for married persons, you know. Every strength and weakness of character is exposed; the stresses of daily work, the joys and sorrows of life provide a constant testing ground. In sickness and in health, in good fortune and through bad times, a married pair must sustain each other and help each other grow spiritually.

**Augustine:** But a married couple do not give each other spiritual direction or confess to one another.

**Mary:** Perhaps not in a formal fashion. But well-married people do confess and apologize to each other constantly and receive an assurance of their spouse's love and forgiveness. It is impossible for imperfect human beings not to fail those around them in subtle or not so subtle ways. In a good and equal marriage where communication is free and open between the partners you learn of your failures immediately. That's one of the reasons women must be equal in power in the home and in the marriage, so that there can be an ideal situation for open honest speech. Ideally in a marriage one should never fear to speak up or have to worry about being scorned or ridiculed—or in worse cases for women, the fear of being beaten. Each spouse can then give reasons and opinions and be open to persuasion about the most important and central personal issues of life.

Other friends and those with whom you work outside the household may only see your more controlled and public presentations and thoughts—and certain concerns remain off limits. But at home, in every conceivable interaction, in bed and out, in good health and ill health, in work and play, in triumph and in despair, a spouse can know and communicate with you in as intimate way as is possible on this earth. And in a loving marriage you have the strongest of all motivations to live virtuously and be sorry when you fail. In countless experiences in marriage you come to know yourself.

**Augustine:** Of course we can never really know ourselves fully. What a mystery the human mind and person is! I have always said that I do not understand how persons can seek to understand the external world and yet not pay more attention to the inner depths and unknown workings of the mind. I wonder how married partners could manage to plumb the depths of each other's being.

**Mary:** I agree that no one ever knows another completely, and we humans only know our selves when we meet the Lord face-to-face. But we can see the flaws and faults of those we live with. More happily we also see their virtues and strengths. We can see how the people we know best struggle to be good—how kind and thoughtfully they can act in small ways as well as at moments of crisis. Ordinary love produces strength as well as confident joy and hope.

A spouse who is a best friend can support you in new and risky enterprises. So many people would never try new kinds of work, or defy worldly opinion in order to fight a current evil, without the support of a loving spouse. If your most intimate friend and marital partner believes in you and your actions, who can discourage you? A husband or wife who is a friend and equal can help a spouse to scale great heights—whether in the world or in spiritual development. The Lord, as our friend, gives us strength to do greater works than we could imagine, and a mate who is a soul friend can also inspire us to imagine a better life.

**Augustine:** I do remember as one of the most sweet and marvelous moments of my life a conversation about heaven and spiritual things that I had with my dear mother Monica shortly before she died. There in that room in Ostia looking down on the courtyard, we talked of our dearest hopes and dreams of God's plan for human beings. We felt inspired and transported in our mutual Christian hope and vision of heavenly truths.

**Mary:** Yes, when we were with the Lord we often felt our hearts burn within us. As with the disciples on the road to Emmaus, Christ's presence and the effect he has upon us, can inspire and transform our lives. I remember how as we talked with him and ate with him, we felt such friendship and joy that we felt we were already in the Kingdom of heaven. After we fully accepted the Resurrection and the Good News that Christ is with us always, even our fears of death and persecution were overcome. With Christ in us we could turn the world upside down. Our new lives in the new creation and Kingdom had already begun for us as a community. I'm convinced that each of us is created for communion and to partake of the marriage banquet of the Lord in the company of the saints.

So we begin here on earth to enjoy and encourage one another in our table fellowship, in our heart-to-heart talks, and become brave enough to try and create a world lived in accord with the gospel. Just as in your experience with Monica and with your friends, so married people and families encourage one another and create a small civilization of love, or a cell of the Church.

And remember, two married people may talk with one another for decades and decades. Marital gossip and recounting of the day's events, and the children's doings and the news of the day is important. I know you hate gossip and wrote on your dining table "no gossiping," but I am sure you meant malicious gossip. Other kinds of gossip or comment upon behavior, such as you often gave in your lively sermons, can be a moral force; it can help sustain and further our consensus about the norms and "oughts" that should govern our life in common. Who wants to lose the respect of those we admire most? Daily conversations not only strengthen a couple's mutual bond and intimate friendship, but as they talk and interpret the world around them, they create the social reality that becomes the small commonwealth of their home.

Each marriage builds up a society with its own customs, rules and outlook. In a Christian marriage a Church in the home is created that will not only give birth to, nurture and educate new members, but shelter and comfort them. Family worship and prayer can sustain the larger Church by creating anew in each generation a Christian community. Families not only give hospitality to others, but some marital partners can be called to go forth with confidence and courage on Christian missions to change the world. Many married pairs, like the early apostles Prisca and Acquila, can be successful in evangelizing for the Kingdom.

**Augustine:** You make me glad that I have written so much in praise of marriage and the necessity for stable marriages in building the city of God. Granted, from your perspective, my ideals of marriage and family may have been too Roman and not near enough to your ideal of an equal marital friendship that could be free and emotionally open.

But even if you reject Roman patriarchy and hierarchical order, don't you admit that the Stoic philosophers were wise to hold up the ideal of achieving rational self-control over the passions? Not only have I felt the most pain and bitterness from erotic love, but even in family life and in my attachments to my friends, I have felt so much grief when I lost them. I felt ashamed of my uncontrolled grief over my mother's death. In her strong faith she was ready to die and possess the joy of being with Christ. I was the one who wept and could not share in her happiness.

**Mary:** But how could you not have shed tears? Such sorrows arising from the bonds of love are an unavoidable part of the human condition. You, dear Augustine, who show yourself so understanding of God's ardent love for us, should recognize that God is tenderhearted toward our human emotions.

**Augustine:** But after the triumph of Christ over death, should not we as rational souls be strong enough to overcome our emotions of sorrow and continued longing for our loved ones who die?

**Mary:** Well, those Stoic philosophers you read did recommend rational detachment from any and all emotional bonds. They believed if a man could prove himself completely detached and without any desires he could rationally master himself and so transcend whatever fate might bring. One can hear that an esteemed classical philosopher accepted the news of the death of his son with complete stoic equanimity by saying, "I did not think that I had fathered an immortal." I know that you criticize the Stoics for their un-Christian ideals, but there still seems to linger in your writing some self-criticism for your grief over your mother's death, or your son's passing, or the loss of your dear friends.

Remember how Jesus wept over Lazarus' death and how troubled in spirit and sorrowfully compassionate he was on so many different occasions. How he praised the emotional excesses of the penitent woman who showed her love and gratitude for him by washing his feet with her tears and wiping them with her unbound hair. This was a scandalous, excessive exhibition of emotion in front of everyone, and it brought Jesus' commendation for the intensity of her loving. In your mourning and tears for your lost loved ones, I do not think you are untrue to the Lord we know and love.

**Augustine:** Yes, I, too, mention Jesus weeping for Lazarus as well as his other real emotions, such as his yearning to eat the Passover with his disciples or his angry grief at man's hardness of heart. But in our Lord's case he only "displayed these feelings in situations where he decided that they should be shown."⁴ While Jesus displayed real human emotions he only "accepted those emotions in his human mind for the sake of his fixed providential design, when he so decided."⁵ By contrast, we as weak humans feel emotions when we do not want to, against our will—often when the emotions are not right. But even when they are right these disturbing emotions belong only to this life—"this place of misery."

**Mary:** I cannot agree with you that Jesus Christ only felt emotions when "he decided to." That is not what happened when he sweat blood on the night of his betrayal. No, his fully human nature meant that he gave himself fully to the human condition without reserve. He did not decide to accept grief, but grieved; he did not just accept compassion, but his very being was moved with compassion for those who suffered. Here again we come to one of those basic disagreements we have been having about human nature and the Good News.

As you have worked all your life annotating the Psalms, don't you see how they are filled with great cries and moans and celebratory shouts of every human emotion?

**Augustine:** Yes, but these passions and desires are directed to God and they take place in our fallen state. In paradise I believe human beings would only have experienced calm, serene tranquil emotions—serene sex, calm gladness, even perhaps serene fear. We would not have felt any frivolous jollity in paradise. And so, as it was in paradise, it will be in heaven. I believe that we will experience only calm gladness again.

**Mary:** No frivolous jollity in Paradise?! I can only assure you, dear Augustine, that Jesus was witty, joyful and delightfully playful. Don't you hear his wit in his parables? How can you imagine God not being playful and merry? Look at the creation, and at babies. Maybe this insight into delight, merriment and wit is one of those things that you might well have learned more thoroughly from women and children.

You are right when you say "for to be sure, just as an especially violent emotion is reflected in the countenance so that inward meditations are to some extent recognized outwardly by men, so it should not be incredible if even milder thoughts afford some indications through the medium of the body."[6] And these are the signs of feeling that as embodied humans we read in one another. And the more we love one another, the more emotionally attuned and sensitive we become to others. The wisdom to read the hearts of others arises in our own hearts.

So you should be thankful that you weep often and, like me, possess the gift of tears. Despite your words you show yourself to be too tender and passionate to completely repress your feelings. Your enemies might say that you were always too relentless like your mother and passionately aggressive like your father to ever have become a stoic. While you may berate every involuntary desire and feeling you have experienced, you keep having them anyway. I also notice that you make an exception and never worry over emotional excess when it comes to your passionate love of God, your intense desires for learning, or your intense sense of guilt over your sins. All those who have read your *Confessions* have been deeply moved by your intimate disclosures of your intense inner emotional life.

**Augustine:** Yes, but remember my account in my *Confessions* of how as a young man at the theater I would weep because I wanted to weep. And how I was in love

106

with love and so fell into a sinful life. Or how I note the sad fact that people love to look at mangled corpses for the titillation and thrill of it—just as they like to go to the violent gladiatorial games. Believe me, I know that our human emotions, too, can be used in self-deceptive ways. We can manipulate ourselves and others with emotional displays just as we lie with words and deeds.

**Mary:** Dear Augustine, how incorrigible you are in your pessimistic view of humankind and in your fear of self-deception and lying. I think you are too severe and stringent in your interpretations of both God and humankind, but in your relentlessness, you have worn me down. Let me take some time to renew my energies for the last sessions of our demanding dialogue. Until tomorrow.

## For Reflection

- *How have I tried to speak up in friendship when I thought I should admonish and correct my partner? What worked and what failed?*

- *How have I made progress in being able to receive correction of my faults and failings without resentment and petulance? If and when I have resisted unpleasant news, what did this reveal to me about myself?*

- *As a couple how have we worked at the art of open communication so that we can disagree and work toward solutions of differences? How have we handled conflict? Is there a more creative and truly Christian way to do this in our marriage?*

- *In what ways might our shared prayer help us to hold fast to Christ who is the peace between us? How has our mutual commitment to Christ enabled us to grow together in marriage?*

## *Closing Prayer*

If your delight is in souls, love them in God, because they too are frail and stand firm only when they cling to him. If they do not, they go their own way and are lost. Love them, then in him and draw as many with you to him as you can. Tell them "He is the one we should love. He made the world and he stays close to it." For when he made the world he did not go away and leave it. By him it was created and in him it exists. Where ever we taste the truth, God is there. He is in our very inmost hearts, but our hearts have strayed from him. Think well on it, unbelieving hearts and cling to him who made you. Stand with him and you shall not fall; rest in him and peace shall be yours.[7]

## *Notes*

[1] *Confessions*, Book I, 8, p. 29.

[2] Augustine, *City of God*, Book XIV, trans. Henry Bettenson (New York: Penguin Classics, 1984), p. 555.

[3] Gerard Manley Hopkins, "Thou art indeed just, Lord, if I contend," *Poems*, 3rd ed. (New York: Oxford University Press, 1948), p. 113.

[4] *City of God*, Book XIV, Chapter 9, p. 563.

[5] Ibid., p. 564.

[6] Augustine, *The Divination of Demons*, trans. Ruth Wentworth Brown, Ph.D., in *The Fathers of the Church: A New Translation*, Vol. 27 (New York: The Fathers of the Church, Inc., 1955), p. 431.

[7] *Confessions*, Book IV, 12, p. 82.

# Day Six
## Learning to Face the Darkness

### Coming Together in the Spirit

A wise old widow I knew once told me of her efforts to save her marriage. Her tale took place in the 1960's when, out of the blue, her heretofore faithful husband in his mid-fifties suddenly became infatuated with a young married colleague and wanted out of his marriage. After thirty-two years of a loving marriage with many grown-up children, my friend was instantly cast into a state of heartbreak and crisis.

In those days the Church offered little practical guidance on how to stay married, especially when your partner spurns you. So my friend, who was a devout reader as well as a devout Catholic, turned to her favorite Henry James novel, *The Golden Bowl*. Its heroine, Maggie Verver, could offer my friend inspiration and hope because Maggie rises to a marital crisis of infidelity and overcomes disaster.

Maggie, who is a nineteenth-century American heiress, has traveled abroad with her widowed father and married a handsome, charming but impoverished Italian prince. Maggie adores her husband and they have a beloved child. But her happiness is overthrown when she accidentally finds out that her handsome prince is having an affair. Worse still, the other woman is Maggie's old school friend, Charlotte, who has recently wed Maggie's beloved millionaire father.

When Maggie learns of the affair, she resolves to save her marriage without ruining her father's happiness or losing her adored husband. Maggie is a Catholic, but just like my elderly friend, she could not turn to her confessor for much help on how to proceed. Should she remain silent, ignore the adultery and passively put up with the lies and deceptions of her husband and her father's wife? No. Instead, Maggie determines to overcome evil while doing no harm.

When Maggie obtains proof that the prince and Charlotte have been lovers, she hotly confronts the prince and reveals her knowledge, along with her hurt and her moral indignation at the double betrayal of herself and her father. But she speaks out only one time to make her demands for change perfectly clear.

Maggie courageously continues to behave beautifully and waits for her prince to decide on his course of action. When Maggie's father intuitively seems to understand the situation, he quietly announces that he will take Charlotte back home to America.

The price to be paid for the separation is Maggie's pain at the loss of her father, and her father's loss of both his daughter and his beloved grandson. On the day after the older couple sail, Maggie waits breathlessly to find out the fate of her own marriage. In a dramatic moment she finds that her beloved prince is awed by her strength and magnanimity; he loves her more ardently than ever. Both partners have grown wiser and their marriage bond stronger.

My friend took Maggie as her model and resisted the temptation to make a public denunciation of her husband's betrayal. Such an act would have wreaked personal and professional havoc for him and his lover. But in private my friend spoke out to her husband in vigorous moral protest and demanded that he change his behavior if the marriage was to continue. Then, like Maggie, she waited and silently suffered in obsessive grief; she told me that this was the most intense psychic pain that she had ever known. She was horribly jealous and deeply hurt by his rejection of her, and she was disillusioned that her husband could behave so callously and in such contradiction to all his previous principles.

Worst of all she herself was repeatedly tempted to take revenge. As she noted, rage at being betrayed in love brings out the violence and unconverted depths of the heart. My friend said that often she had to cling to Christ as her saving anchor against the temptation to wound those who had wounded her. A wave of bitter hostility and desire to do harm would rise up and almost engulf her, and only recede with time and prayer.

In her distress my friend prayed for forbearance and the courage to forgive her husband. She meditated on the betrayal of Jesus, the uses of suffering and constantly invoked the Lord's help in her efforts to maintain hope for her marriage. My friend had to endure a multitude of horrible, but completely private, marital scenes marked by cruel emotional abuse. Yet, at the same time, the public family routine and polite external face of the marriage continued—even with moments of affectionate intimacy. In this schizophrenic situation my friend had to withstand sessions in which her guilt-ridden husband tried to blame, shame and grievously destroy her sense of self. "I never loved you," or "you have no friends," and so on. Since my friend had many loving friends and much evidence to refute these crazed accusations, she managed to keep her grip on reality. But her sense of survival and hope for a reconciliation could only be maintained by countless disciplined acts of self-control and pleas to God for help.

Eventually the marital tornado passed without blowing the family apart. Like Maggie, my friend had saved her marriage from a severe case of male midlife crisis. Gradually after a decade or so, the marriage recovered, and the couple spent a mutually supportive old age until in his eighties her husband died of a stroke. In Henry James's words my friend had "seen her husband through." A family breakdown was averted by a strong legacy from previous marital harmony and my friend's faith and commitment to fidelity. Her children and grandchildren never knew the story she told me; they were only edified by the example of such a good marriage that endured for fifty-nine years—for better or worse, until death did them part.

## Defining Our Thematic Context

Living out a lifetime of marital fidelity requires not only a readiness to enjoy and celebrate love's gifts, but the willingness and the toughness to endure, suffer and overcome difficulties. How this is to be done remains an open question of prudence and judgment. Since no blueprint works for everyone or every unique marital relationship, Christians must become "shrewd as a serpent, innocent as a dove."

Indeed, all successful and happy families are happy in their own way. Tolstoy's famous opening lines to *Anna Karenina*[1] must be reversed, because it is the unhappy families which are alike in their doleful failures of love. Yet God is always faithful and in long marriages we slowly learn to love one another as God has loved us.

## Opening Prayer

Lord, deliver us from the snare of evil hate. Give us faithfulness as a shield and buckler against betrayal and abuse. When we are injured grant us the strength to forgive the other as we have been forgiven. Never let us lose hope in love's reconciling power. Endlessly enkindle the fires of our desire for love and endow us with the courage to endure to the end.

# Retreat Session Six

**Mary:** Let me begin by admitting to you, dear Augustine, and to our retreatants that I have avoided discussing the potential sufferings of marriage. I have done so because I believe that among Christians the discussion of marriage and sexuality has been too biased by pessimism, much of it, I might say, springing from the powerful influence through the ages of Augustinian ideas.

Yet, I, too, recognize that marriage can be the source of great suffering and disappointment—just because intimacy possesses so much potential for reward. The more possibility there is to experience with a mate friendship, passion, joy, support and mutual encouragement, the more it hurts to fail. Was it not ever thus with marriage? The accounts of marriage and family life in our ancient Hebrew Scriptures reveal so many instances of jealousy, vengeance, deception, favoritism, ambition, incest, rape, sexual abuse and violence in the relationships between men and women, in and out of the family. In biblical accounts both men and women sin and err with disastrous results. The antipathy and hostility that can exist between the sexes becomes sadly clear.

**Augustine:** Yes, my dear lady, facing these facts honestly will move you toward my more realistic position.

**Mary:** Well, you know that I disagree with you on your view of the consequences of original sin. While our human nature is flawed and wounded, it is not as depraved as you think. In Christian marriage men and women can at last overcome the hostility, the competitiveness and the distrust that has been called the war between the sexes. In fact, in a just and equal married friendship, all the previous bad experiences that a person may have had with the opposite sex, in their family and in their youth, can be healed.

All that rejection, scorn, envy or competitive anxiety that men and women have felt for each other can fall away in an intimate loving relationship. Cooperating in family life calls forth the full range of personal qualities of each spouse. After a long marriage many persons find that the old mystique of a distant "opposite sex" dissolves in appreciation of a mate's individual qualities and character. A "neighboring sex" perhaps? When we were in the company of the Lord we disciples felt this same liberating freedom from confining categories of class, gender or race. Past suspicions, fears and prejudices that had once divided us were made one in Christ's unity.

**Augustine:** I have always seen the inner self and a person's unique consciousness in God as the greatest mystery in the creation. And the unity of wills and mutual personal commitment of the marriage bond encompass every dimension of a person, be they male or female. In Christ there is neither slave nor free, male nor female, Jew nor Greek. Becoming one in Christ heals all of our divisions and hostilities. Yes, I have always maintained that the equal mutual faithfulness and commitment between a married pair is one of the three great goods of marriage. If we are faithful to God we will be faithful to each other.

**Mary:** I agree with your teaching that this fidelity of marriage supports that other great good of marriage, the gift of children. But I think we should add something for our retreatants that you leave out, perhaps because of the early death of your son; one of the greatest joys of marriage and procreation is seeing one's children happily married and producing a third generation of grandchildren. And I am sure that seeing an example of marital fidelity in one's parents helps a younger generation believe in marriage and so stay married for the sake of their own children.

Yes, no matter what the age of offspring, it is important for them to see a strong marital bond between their parents. The security of permanent marriage commitments is a good of marriage for a couple, but it allows children to grow up with the assurance that they will always have two parents. They can be supported by two families of kin invested in rearing them and launching them into adulthood; the extended family and loving kinship group is a great blessing.

**Augustine:** True, but you also must recognize that you will bear the sorrows of your children's troubles and their children's sufferings. But obviously we need stable families for support and order.

**Mary:** Back we go to order, order, order. I prefer the judgment of a saint from Ireland who was a zealous missionary helping restore the Church after the barbarians had destroyed Roman civilization. He said "Love has nothing to do with order."[2] A living love will be creative and spontaneous; life with people brings disorder as new opportunities to respond keep burgeoning and springing up within a person and within a good relationship. Let's not confuse commitment and faithfulness with rigidity and inflexibility.

**Augustine:** Well, if I concede that perhaps I have made too much of the need for order, will you not say more about your admission that many sufferings can accompany marriage? I notice you slid away from that topic rather quickly.

**Mary:** I do know and recognize that the betrayal of love in a marriage is one of the greatest hurts that a human being can experience.

One of the greatest sorrows that I saw Jesus experience was the desertion, defection and betrayal of his closest friends. It also hurt him when he was rejected by those religious believers who should have most welcomed him and discerned the truth of his message; they even leveled false accusations of impiety against him.

Those Christians suffering in marital storms can remember what Christ suffered from his friends and contemporaries. Remembering Christ's example and his teachings, I think we can take heart from the promise that our sufferings can be used by God. Many men and women who have borne their marital crosses bravely for Christ's sake, offer them to God and believe that they help the Kingdom come.

**Augustine:** Always Christ's triumph over evil and sin is central to our Christian faith. Alas, I have seen so much sin and suffering among my congregations. Infidelity and harm done to women from sexual sins and abuses is a great and prevalent evil. And to be fair, and no way biased against women, I must also report that I have seen wives who caused their husbands much suffering.

**Mary:** Yes, abuses of power in a marriage can hurt so much. And of course there are many forms of power. In bad marriages there can be physical abuse, physical desertion, sexual and financial exploitation, and acts of cruelty of a very crude kind. These sins often are associated with the sin of drunkenness that you inveigh against. Often it takes spouses in a bad marriage a long time before they can finally admit that their expectations are not going to be met and that they will not be able to fulfill their dreams. Then there is the next stage when in certain dreadful situations a marriage cannot be endured without grievous harm, and it breaks down completely. As you teach, sometimes separation may be the only solution for dreadful situations.

But in better marriages, and even in good marriages that endure, there also can be sorrows and distress arising from more subtle problems. And I do not refer only to the hardships of bearing and rearing children, or economic struggles, or growing old or ill together or facing the deaths of children. Some sorrows come not from outside but from within the marriage itself.

**Augustine:** I do not follow your meaning here. As you know, I have admitted that I will never understand the mystery of marriage, and perhaps this is an example of an obscure point which I cannot grasp.

**Mary:** Unfortunately, while change can be creative in a marriage, often it can bring problems. A couple must develop together in order to avoid growing apart.

Ideological differences and divergence of interests may become more pronounced as people mature and pursue different worlds. Silences which can be so companionable in a good marriage can become cold silences of indifference or boredom. Or perhaps one person refuses to grow. And when there is a change or reversal in central moral values, or a lapse in religious beliefs, great pain over the differences between a couple can appear. The earlier unity of living as one heart and mind can be mourned. There may be no outright betrayal, abuse, infidelity or desertion involved, but there can be sorrow when one spouse can no longer accompany the other on their spiritual journey.

**Augustine:** And what do you recommend in these times of distress, whether facing such subtle or more serious difficulties?

**Mary:** Here Christians can truly take refuge in God and be sustained and comforted by faith. Constant prayer, worship and efforts to grow up into Christ our head can help transform a distressing situation. God never fails; Christ is our rock from whom living waters of comfort and transformation flow. I think spouses should always go the second mile, but never allow themselves to be treated in a way that injures their inherent human dignity as a child of God. Speaking up and working for a just solution is as necessary in marriage and family life as it is in other communities faced with conflict or distress. But sometimes the problems can be so subtle. Seeking the wisdom of God, a spouse seeks to save the marriage and the well-being of the family. Taking counsel from the wise and developing strong friendships or working for others in one's community can help to sustain a spouse during periods of severe marital stress.

**Augustine:** I have had to counsel some married couples on the problems that arise when one person in the marriage, in most cases the woman, wishes to become more spiritually committed and the other spouse does not. One prominent rich woman, Euvodia, wished to quit sexual relations, refuse all wifely and domestic duties, move apart from her husband, no longer take his name and give away her children's patrimony to charity. I told her that all of these actions were wrong because it betrayed her vow of commitment to her husband and broke the bond of faithfulness in the marital union. In her misguided enthusiasm she disregarded her husband's feelings and his spiritual welfare; when his protests were futile he was driven away from home and ended up in an adulterous relationship. To unilaterally break a marriage, even in order to be more spiritually devoted was wrong— as was giving away her children's money. I advised her to write to her husband and ask his forgiveness, tell him to return home and work to restore their marital unity.

**Mary:** Ah, how much going forth and coming back home there must be for marriages to endure. Forgiveness and reconciliation is central to the vocation of Christian marriage. It is just as important to be able to forgive as to receive forgiveness in your turn—much harder for some proud types. Married persons who follow Jesus and never return evil for evil can have a chance to overcame evil by love. Jesus taught us that God truly fulfills the promise, "A bruised reed I will not break or a flickering wick quench." Otherwise, love and charity have no chance to grow fruitful through forbearance and forgiveness. Paul was wise when he advised Christians never to let the sun set on their anger. Perhaps no one can actually forget past injuries, that might be imprudent or unsafe; and sometimes married people must seek separation or legal redress, but forgive we must. We forgive by restoring the relationship of goodwill toward those who injure us—even if they don't ask forgiveness, or even if they are no longer alive or present.

If married persons continue to harbor hate or anger against a spouse, it will destroy their ability to receive God's forgiveness and their power to forgive others and enjoy the peace of Christ. Love always means saying you are sorry, and beginning anew to amend your life. This is the main way that a married couple will grow in holiness, or mutual sanctification; living together in loving intimacy is so hard and so challenging that married love can take the place of exotic ascetic practices dreamed up by solitary hermits who had fled their families.

**Augustine:** This view of charity seems very sound Christian doctrine to me, although I think your sally against hermits and ascetic practices unwarranted. Married people also can practice asceticism if both agree. I teach as Paul did before me that married persons should practice continence only with mutual consent. I have taught that if one individual in the marriage wishes to live continently he or she should never refuse the other, while making sure that he or she is never the one to request the sexual act.

**Mary:** Augustine, Augustine, what a repellent piece of advice! Can you imagine what it does to marital unity to be the partner, either husband or wife, who is put into the supplicant's position? It curdles the spirit in marriage to be the one who must always ask and receive sex performed as a duty. Knowing that your partner is reluctant produces great pain. Sometimes reluctant compliance is more wounding than other kinds of blunt refusals. Desire and love wither in the wake of a marital stinginess that produces humiliation and a feeling of rejection.

**Augustine:** Well, I have always taught Saint Paul's words that God loves a glad giver; both pagans and Christians teach that generosity and magnanimity is a virtue. But should we apply this virtue to sexual relationships in marriage?

**Mary:** Rekindling the fire and a ready sexual courtesy and response to one's partner is needed, not reluctant sexual acquiescence given as a duty.

**Augustine:** What I see as spiritual progress in the gift of mutual continence you see as a decline of unity through the waning and neglect of sexual desire. I think spiritual health and integrity comes from dousing the fires of sexual passion while you wish to rekindle them. How can we be so different in our understanding of these matters?

You are forcing me to wonder for the first time whether I have been limited by my own experience which was so negative and harmful. And yes, I can see that I was also a young man when I had the worst of my sexual difficulties. After all, in one's youth it is more likely that sexual desire is most pressing, perpetually at the ready and most likely to become separated from all of the goals of life. It is also more likely that in such circumstances, at least in my world, it is easier for men to disregard the woman and her wishes and desires. So sexuality could more easily be identified with lust and exploitation than with love. Even when women were recognized to have sexual desires and experience sexual pleasure, it was generally thought to be disgusting. But your views, like the poem by Ausonius to his beloved wife, are making me think that ascetic bishops like Ambrose and Roman philosophers of my day could hardly know of the intimate sexual life of all marital partners.

Theoretically I have understood that sexual interest, along with all the rest of our capacities, tends to wane in old age. But since continent marriages have been my ideal, I could hardly see the cooling of desire as a sorrow or problem for married people. Since my own struggles have all been in suppressing sexual desires, I could hardly imagine the opposite problem.

Yet, I have maintained that it is the unity of the human will that is damaged by the fall of human nature. Just as involuntary sexual desires rise again and again despite our efforts to suppress and control them, so I hold that involuntary impotence and failure of willed sexual acts should be seen as part of the punishment inherited from Adam and Eve.

Inconstancy of my desires for God has caused me much sorrow; I have bemoaned the unreliability of my ardor for God and God's holiness. At times my longing for God is intense and real, but then it can fade and become faint. Perhaps I can see from these experiences how, from your perspective, marriage can face similar difficulties in keeping ardent love alive.

**Mary:** Unfortunately, the woundedness of human nature means that no familiar long-married spouse can ever offer the romantic excitement of a new partner with whom one can relive the dramatic opening acts of courtship. Human curiosity and restlessness ensure that people will be enticed by their expectations for a new and initially enthralling sexual passion. Much infidelity springs from the ease with which marriage partners flag in their efforts not to take each other for granted. A marriage suffers when a couple becomes insensitive to the need to continually converse and court an intimate delight in one another as a mysterious creation made in the image of God. Even a long and successful marriage almost always endures cycles of positive and negative periods of enthusiasm, boredom, appreciation and irritation. Marital love is like all the other loves in which Christians must exercise patience and hope.

Paul expresses Christ's will for married love so well when he says:

> Love is patient; love is kind; love is not envious or boastful or arrogant or rude. It does not insist on its own way; it is not irritable or resentful; it does not rejoice in wrongdoing, but rejoices in the truth. It bears all things, believes all things, hopes all things, endures all things.
>
> Love never ends. (*1 Corinthians 13:4-8*)

**Augustine:** My own life has been full of so much conflict and struggle on every side, with enemies without and enemies within. I have always known that life is a hard pilgrimage full of suffering and evil. Disputes and conflicts plagued me to my dying day. And my final days on earth were shadowed by the atrocities of barbarian invasions. In this evil time Christians had to be ready to suffer persecution for their faith, perhaps even to accept torture and martyrdom. As always those who are married and have families will be most vulnerable. For me, true lasting delights and sweetness lie only in heaven. In every harsh experience I was persuaded anew that my hope of complete happiness had to be centered on the living God of my life, my goodness, my sweetness, the fountain of mercy.

**Mary:** Yes, I understand how important your vocation as a dedicated and ascetic friend of God could be in a time of persecution. Your pessimism about life's journey received nothing but confirmation in the increasing violence marking the decline of Roman civilization. Perhaps I might share your bleak views of this world if I had only lived through my violent era with the crucifixion as evidence of the world's dark triumph of evil. But having been healed and made whole, and having met the risen Lord in the garden of an earthly Jerusalem, I cannot be so sure that every Christian life must be marked by constant combat and intense ascetic suffering and struggle. I believe I have been more deeply imbued than you seem to be by the joy, victory and delight given to us here and now in the wondrous Resurrection of my Rabboni. I do not give up on happiness in the present world; many joys are possible in marriage even though struggles and sorrows will be present. Every childbirth takes effort and every creation of a marriage takes struggle, but what delight can ensue, even in this world before the final fulfillment of the Kingdom. All the way to heaven is heaven. Remember we await the coming of the Kingdom in *joyful* hope.

**Augustine:** Amen, amen to that, although I would also have to remind you that all the way to hell is hell. I choose to put the stress somewhat differently, and say that a Christian awaits the Kingdom in joyful *hope*.

And perhaps if we exercise the virtue of hope enough we will come to some resolution of our differences. After all, tomorrow is our last day of dialogue in our retreat. So peace to you, dear friend, until we meet again.

## For Reflection

- *How have I handled disappointments and difficulties with my partner? How have prayer and worship helped me overcome problems in learning to love?*

- *How have I maintained Christian hope when life seemed full of sorrow and trials?*

- *What experiences of giving and receiving forgiveness have helped renew my loving relationships? How was peace restored? Peace maintained?*

- *What examples of Christian loving have kept me faithful to my commitments? How have we as a couple grown together and increased in unity?*


## *Closing Prayer*

When spirits fall, their darkness is revealed, for they are stripped of the garment of your light. By the misery and restlessness which they then suffer you make clear to us how noble a being is your rational creation, for nothing less than yourself suffices to give it rest and happiness. This means that it cannot find them in itself. For you, our God, will shine on the darkness about us. From you proceeds our garment of light, and our dusk shall be noonday.

Give yourself to me, my God restore yourself to me. I show you my love, but if it is too little, give me strength to love you more. I cannot measure its shortcomings and learn how much more I need to love you in order that my life may hasten to your embrace and never turn away from you until it is hidden in the sanctuary of your presence. All that I know is this, that unless you are with me, and not only beside me but in my very self, for me there is nothing but evil, and whatever riches I have, unless they are my God they are only poverty.[3]

## Notes

[1] "Happy families are all alike; every unhappy family is unhappy in its own way." See Leo Tolstoy, trans. Constance Garnett, *Anna Karenina* (New York: Book-of-the-Month Club, Inc., 1991), p. 1.

[2] Abbot Columbanus, quoted in Thomas Cahill, *How The Irish Saved Civilization* (New York: Anchor Books, 1995), p. 176. Cahill suggests that Irish Christianity was more open to diversity and dissent because it was not influenced by Augustine's thought on sexuality and the need for state coercion.

[3] *Confessions*, Book XIII, 8, p. 316.

# Day Seven
## Persevering in Love

### Coming Together in the Spirit

Endurance and patience over long years can bring a difficult marriage to a peaceful and fruitful conclusion. Consider the account of Abraham and Sarah's longlasting marriage found in Genesis. From the beginning of their time together as a couple they wandered far from their native territory. As aliens and immigrants they confronted a host of external dangers, as well as internal marital troubles brought on by their flawed humanity.

Although God promises Abraham many descendants, the beautiful Sarah remains barren and passes beyond the age of childbearing without an infant of her own. Then God does a great deed and vindicates Abraham's faith in the improbable promise. The Lord comes to Abraham and Sarah's tent, accepts their hospitality and proclaims that by the next year Sarah will bear a child. Abraham, thinking on how very old he and Sarah are, falls on his face and laughs, as does Sarah who stands within the tent and overhears the word of the Lord. How can this be? Yet in their old age the impossible happens and Sarah and Abraham produce a son, who is named Isaac, "he who laughs."

Jews, Muslims and Christians count their descent from the prophet Abraham and his wife Sarah; they revere

Abraham's obedience and continuing acts of faith in the Lord's promises. Steadfast faith and the improbable fruitfulness of one elderly married couple's sexual union engenders offspring as numerous as the stars in the sky "from whom all the nations of the earth shall gain blessing."

Admittedly, at first hearing the Lord's promise of a pregnancy, Sarah had laughed and asked herself, "After I have grown old, and my husband is old, shall I have pleasure?" And the Lord hearing her question had given the answer, "Is anything too wonderful for the Lord?" When pleasure and sexual fruitfulness are granted to Sarah and Abraham, Sarah expresses her joy with the words, "God has brought laughter for me; everyone who hears will laugh with me." And to this day, among her descendants God's gift of marriage, love, sexual pleasure and fruitfulness continue to inspire laughter and joy.

### Defining Our Thematic Context

While human frailty, sin and external misfortunes are a part of married life, patient endurance and faith can lead to happiness. Betrayals and abuses of power in marriages can be overcome. Married Christians learn to endure and rejoice; to suffer defeats and to savor triumphs. Above all they learn that love is stronger than death.

### Opening Prayer

Lord, let us be patient. Help us to endure and to hope in you, to take comfort in your love for us. The promise of our transformation by the power of the Holy Spirit cheers our hearts. Our praise and thanksgiving for all your goodness renews our efforts to follow you day by day. In the turbulence of our lives you are our rock in whom our homes and hearts can be grounded. Let our hearts expand through your love so that we can grow in our love for others.

# Retreat Session Seven

**Augustine:** So where have we come in this wandering dialogue of ours? After circling around our topics it is obvious that we have not agreed on many crucial points. Can our different perspectives and special insights be reconciled in some way that makes sense?

**Mary:** I have thought about this problem and come up with some ways that our retreatants can make use of our conflicting views. In a real sense the differences between us point to a basic tension that always exists in the Christian life. Christianity preaches Christ's victory over sin and death, *but* promises that a struggle will be necessary before God's Kingdom comes in its full glory; this contradiction has been called living with "the already and the not yet." We know Christ has conquered and God will be all in all, but in the meantime we still have to work out our salvation in fear and trembling.

You warn against self-deception and sin, and point out the sacrificial cost and discipline of a seriously devout life in a hostile world. I, by contrast, affirm the Good News that in the victory Christ has won for us, our graced creation and human nature give us joy and support. Sexuality and marriage can be a specially graced way to holiness, happiness and joy. In other words, while I do not deny sin, sorrow and the suffering of this world, I want to emphasize for our retreatants the good news about marriage and sexuality—since this view has much too often been neglected by Christians in the past.

**Augustine:** In all honesty, as a responsible Christian pastor, I would have to caution our retreatants who marry, as well as those who do not, that they will have to struggle with deep wells of sinful rebellion existing within themselves. What I say about all sin will apply to married people as well as to everyone else, "Crimes against other men are committed when the emotions which spur us to action are corrupt and rise in revolt without control. Sins of self-indulgence are committed when the soul fails to govern the impulses from which it derives bodily pleasure. In the same way, if the rational mind is corrupt, mistaken ideas and false beliefs will poison life."[1] To become too attached to bodily pleasure, or to a spouse or to one's children, or to any other good thing in the creation deters us in our journey to love. Every Christian, including our retreatants, must be prepared to vigilantly and ceaselessly struggle against pride, self-indulgence and self-deception. Unfortunately, all of God's good things given in the creation can be abused. No matter how holy we have tried to be in our past lives we can never be safe until we are received into heaven.

**Mary:** And I have had to remind our retreatants that while what you maintain is partly true, it is not the whole story. Christians who love others must be passionately attached to their loved ones; just as our God loves us passionately, Christ loved his own. Sexuality and marriage are a blessed part of God's good creation; intense pleasure and ecstasy can give us some small understanding of the intensity and reality of God's blessedness. I want Christians to accept as

God's gift the goodness of passionate erotic loving in the union of marriage and not be afraid or ashamed of their sexuality.

**Augustine:** But my dear Mary, despite your protestations I think it can be argued that sexuality is, if not the most dangerous of all human capacities, at least one of the most dangerous, because it is so powerful and involuntary a desire for self-pleasing consummation. There is always a temptation present in strong human desires for turning from the good and taking pleasure in perverse self-aggrandizement; sexuality, greed and worldly ambitions of all kinds can so easily feed self-will and lead us to rebel against God's will. Persons come to grief if they refuse to rise through love of the lesser to higher loves and the more lasting eternal joys found in God.

**Mary:** My dear Augustine, I do not deny that sexual desires can be abused. But why deny, as you seem to, the God-given goodness of sexual desire and intercourse, even in our fallen human condition?

Well, on second thought, it has occurred to me that our retreatants may view our differences in another way that may be helpful. I think any observer can recognize that you, Augustine, approve wholeheartedly of a human being's ardent desire for God. You write of human delight and fulfillment in God's life, love and joy in powerful words pointing to mystic delights and experiences beyond words.

Therefore, I would point out to our retreatants that I am just taking your wonderful views of God's love for us and our love for God and extending them to passionate sexual love between human beings. You wish to increase the fires of your desire for God and grow in your ability to love your neighbor. And to do so you think you must give up erotic sexual desires. I maintain that erotic sexual loving of one's beloved mate cannot only be a very complete form of charity but a way of understanding and increasing our love of God.

**Augustine:** Dear lady, I admire your efforts to integrate and harmonize our divergent views. You do not convince me in your claim that heaven can begin on earth in passionate sexual pleasures. However, I can point to one small concession I once made to your way of thinking. As you know, in my final years I reread all of my works to see if I should change or correct anything I had once written. And I added one succinct footnote to my treatment on marriage; I say there that "passion in the service of love may not be considered passion."[2]

**Mary:** Of course I am fascinated by that brief and mysterious footnote. I cannot help but think that if you developed that train of thought, you and I would be more likely to agree that the involuntariness of sexual desire and sexual consummation should not be considered negative.

**Augustine:** I am sure you would like to claim that involuntarily and against my will I am, without knowing it, really agreeing with you about sex and passion! No, that would be going too far.

**Mary:** Unfortunately your Christian understanding of the revolutionary equality of women and the goodness of marriage constantly became overlaid by the influences of your own history in your late Roman world.

**Augustine:** Well, my dear lady, your accusations echo the attacks of all of my opponents in one swooping assault.

**Mary:** Forgive me for my open reactions. However much others may disagree with you, all are in awe of your passionate zeal, your acute psychological insight, your brilliant mind grappling with mysteries and your wonderful use of language. You may deplore the dangers of sensual and erotic love in your philosophy but, in the wonderfully ardent language you use for religious experience, you validate the power of eros. So who could resist being disarmed by your charm?

**Augustine:** Thank you, my dear opponent. You know, as I lay dying I shut myself up alone in my room the better to do penance for my past sins. It is only too certain that I failed often and made errors and possessed unacknowledged self-deceptions. Who can know the depths of one's hidden flaws? But I am forever eager to learn more about God's beauty and wisdom which must always astonish us. I would sin against humility and truth if I were not open to correction. I deeply regret whatever may have been incorrect or incomplete in my writings. In a real sense, do not our reconsiderations of God's mysteries go on for the whole of our lives?

**Mary:** Yes, and so as we bring our retreat to a close let us reconsider the extent of our agreements. We both sing of the ineffable graciousness of the love of God and affirm the goods of marriage.

**Augustine:** We certainly agree that everything that is made by God exists in the Lord and shows forth God's goodness. Together we affirm that we must be grateful for all of our wonderful human capacities of body, mind and spirit. Our minds, memories and will can know and act in wondrous ways beyond any of the other animals who lack the gift of reason.

**Mary:** Of course, I would add to this litany of gratitude, thanksgiving for sexual love in marriage. And for playfulness, comedy and the frivolous jollity of human beings, especially that playfulness open to married lovers. Only mammals play, you know, and most of them only play when they are young. It is the glory of human beings that they can continue to play into maturity and old age. Enjoying the wit, comedy and fun of life is vital for everyone's health and well-being and especially so within a marriage. The gravity and seriousness held in esteem by Romans and stoic philosophers is not necessarily a Jewish or Christian ideal. We must not forget to connect playfulness with the love, friendship and lifelong fidelity in marriage.

**Augustine:** I will proceed to the more important fact that in our dialogues we have agreed on the goods of marriage which I enumerate as fidelity, the bond of marital unity and the gift of children. And while I hold virginity to be the higher call, I recognize that the celibate calling can be distorted. It is clear that faithful married people, including married women martyrs like the courageous and greathearted Perpetua and Crispina, can be as holy as those persons dedicated to virginity.

**Mary:** Yes, and I agree that dedicated virginity and celibacy is a great gift to the Church. When celibates give all of their energy and work to build up the Church of God and minister to the needs of the world, everyone benefits.

I also think that dedicated celibates, like faithful married people, give witness to the truth that human sexuality can be directed to increasing our love of God and neighbor. Christians reject those pagan myths that see sexuality as some semi-divine power of nature which must be served at all costs. Sexuality is more like a form of speech, or an expressive nonverbal language. And because human beings have been given rationality, free will and foresight, we can speak and sexually act out only what is true and appropriate. We can also make promises to bind our future behavior. Only human beings made in the image of God can make promises and lovingly fulfill them by freely willed behavior. The human sense of family and moral obligations to kinship is a human attribute based upon the capacity to make promises and be faithful.

**Augustine:** We aspire to be faithful and keep our promises because God is faithful to us. To demand that males be faithful to their wives just as wives must be faithful was a revolutionary demand in my Roman world, you know. Perhaps you would not be satisfied with the pace of change and how long it took for a revolutionary view of women to penetrate Christian thought and civil society, but change began with the gospel.

**Mary:** Yes, Jesus initiated a revolution in protecting the equal dignity of women—and of children. We both agree on women's equal value before the Lord and in the Lord. But as you suspect, you do not go far enough for me. If women are equally valuable and equally friends and "co-heirs" of Christ's Kingdom, then this must mean that men and women exist as equals in the family and have equal powers in civic society and in the Church. If we follow our Lord's liberated and liberating example, women can no longer be identified with the irrational or with natural impulses and so be subjected to the control of men. Much of the prejudice against women arises from fear and that subtle form of discrimination which overemphasizes women's sexuality.

**Augustine:** All such prejudice can be conquered by love. The Christian life is centered on love and friendship. And so we must love our neighbor, our friends, our families and, most difficult of all, our enemies. How difficult I have sometimes found it to love my enemies and to have patience with stubborn and stupid opponents! I have been driven in desperation to pray, "O Life of the poor, O my God, in whose bosom there is no contradiction, I beg you to water my heart with the rain of forbearance, so that I may bear with such people in patience."[3]

**Mary:** But you did not have to contend with so many of the irritations of marital confrontations, which can require more forbearance and patience than public conflicts. A wife or a husband who is truly "another self," provides an intimate challenge to spiritual growth. No one should be afraid to speak up or be silenced in a Christian family, and certainly not those women and children who often possess the least power or worldly status. If the whole Church should be "the world turned inside out" when it comes to exercising power and using talents and gifts for service, then a Christian couple should lead the way in exemplary love and support for one another.

**Augustine:** Yes, and I think I have had a glimmer of the freedom truly to be open with a woman as a friend when I remember those long conversations I had with my mother. I am ashamed to say that once, when she opposed my plan to go to Rome to teach, I resorted to tricking her in order to sail away. I left her, the best of mothers, weeping on the shore.

**Mary:** And would it not have been more difficult to have left your wife behind in that way? But in any event Monica did follow you to Milan. When she was dying

Monica said she could never remember your being anything but the best of sons to her. Family life always teaches us central lessons about forgiveness and reconciling our differences. I so well remember how Jesus told us parable after parable, such as the story of the prodigal son, to make the point that forgiveness, and especially forgiveness within the family even to seventy times seven, is the core of Christian love.

**Augustine:** Yes, how I regret all of those sins and lapses in my life that my good mother did not choose to remember. I felt so much sorrow when she died. When I think how my heart was broken at her death, and my grief at the death of my beloved son, and the wrenching pain of losing my mistress, I wonder. Could I have withstood more intense pains, confrontations and losses involved in a long marriage? Surely the Lord was good to give me my vocation, difficult as it was to follow.

**Mary:** Now, let us make the importance of perseverance our last point for our retreatants. It takes a lifetime to learn to love wholeheartedly and well. We think we love well and then find that we become affronted and irritated when things do not go our way. If our feelings become hurt or our partner flags in love, we, too, are tempted to withdraw and leave frustration behind. Intimacy is a two-edged sword. We become completely familiar with another; every flaw, along with every good quality, becomes magnified by constant observation and interaction. Annoyance and impatience can constantly increase unless we pray and increase in love. Only attending to God's love and mercy to us can renew our fountains of forbearance and kindness.

I always remember how Jesus promised that in God's grace we could have living waters of love flow from our hearts. He made me understand that every moment, and every day should be a Sabbath. In the power of the resurrection of our Lord we can constantly begin again, in renewed loving relationship with our friends, spouses and family members.

Love has no end and perseveres in patience. Even if old age or illness rob married people of sexual intimacy, they can have the privilege of nurturing and nursing each other till death do them part. Love engenders patience and waiting in hope. As James tells us, "Be patient...beloved, until the coming of the Lord. The farmer waits for the precious crop from the earth, being patient with it until it receives the early and the late rains. You also must be patient. Strengthen your hearts, for the coming of the Lord is near.... Indeed we call blessed those who showed endurance. You have heard of the endurance of Job, and you have seen the purpose of the Lord, how the Lord is compassionate and merciful" (James 5:7, 8, 11). Yes, we Christians must see each other through.

**Augustine:** I and all the Church have admired you, Mary, for your steadfastness and patience. You never deserted Jesus and you stood by the cross until death. Your perseverance and determination to find the body of Jesus and do him honor inspire our determination. Nothing could stand in your way. And at the Resurrection you hurried instantly to carry out Christ's wishes and give witness to the Good News.

**Mary:** I can also testify, as I am sure you can, Augustine, my friend, that one of the pains of life is watching those we love suffer and not to be able to succor them. Life in the Church and in the family is replete with vicarious suffering. How often we want to echo Jesus' lament for Jerusalem. How we, too, would love, like a mother hen, to take all our beloved chicks under our wings to give them shelter and comfort. One of the joys of heaven consists in being able to help others forever through the communion of saints.

And for the married saints, steadfast love means suffering with and for the other if need be. In our marriages we should be a joyful sign of the marriage of the Lamb.

## For Reflection

- How has my desire for the love of God and the love of my spouse faded and then been renewed? How were these experiences of renewal associated with Scripture, worship or the life of the Church and the communion of saints?

- What examples of patience and endurance in living a loving Christian life have I experienced?

- What are some of the ways I have found to persevere patiently in my love and commitment to my spouse and family?

- How might this retreat alter or deepen my appreciation of sexuality and marriage?

- To which of our mentors do I feel closer? Why?

## Going Forth

**Mary:** Dear Augustine, in closing our dialogue we must make it clear to our retreatants that they may be finishing a retreat but only beginning the rest of their lives. For Christians there can be no end of loving. Nor as we have demonstrated, will there ever be an end to trying to understand love, sex and marriage.

**Augustine:** I agree that love has no end and that divine love is the ultimate mystery. But I hope that after our humble efforts in these sessions our retreatants will go on reflecting and learning on their own. And if they think it helpful, they can certainly continue to use us as mentors for their spiritual journey. I have written so many books and shorter works and sermons that anyone who wishes to know more of my reflections on living the Christian life can plunge in and read.

I always recommend studying as a way to seek wisdom and increased understanding of our God who is both truth and love. Every turning point in my own spiritual journey was inspired by reading. The words, "Take and read," which I overheard in the garden in Milan and which initiated my conversion, could serve as a maxim for my whole life.

**Mary:** When you recount the story of your conversion, you say that it was at the moment you opened the Bible and your eyes fell upon verses from Saint Paul's Letter to the Romans that by the end of the sentence you felt flooded with the light of confidence and the darkness of doubt was dispelled. Christ the Word spoke to you through the inspired words of Scripture. I don't know whether I would recommend your method of relying on a chance opening of the good book to find the right verse for guidance (too much like magical pagan divination), but I certainly recommend to our retreatants that they seek spiritual growth in the constant reading of all of the New Testament. For ordinary folk, married or unmarried, there's no better way to learn how to love one another than to take to heart the gospel's Good News.

The story of my own encounter with the risen Lord,

also in a garden, can only be found in John's Gospel. But all four of the Gospels mention me as a woman disciple and intimate friend of the Lord who walked with him. Of course our brief New Testament accounts written long after the life of Jesus could never tell the whole amazing story of Christ and the early Church. Silences and omissions exist, especially when it comes to the role of women. But silence about women's presence does not mean that we were not there. It is just that the ordinary background or the usual order of things can be so taken for granted that it is not thought significant enough to be mentioned. Remember at the feeding with the loaves and fishes it was said that four thousand people surrounded Christ, "not counting women and children." Or when Jesus told his disciples to let the children come to him, it isn't pointed out that Jesus was welcoming the women who were carrying their children and trying to get close to him. His tenderness and healing love shone forth so powerfully that he won the hearts of the multitude— especially those of us who often remained invisible and weren't counted.

We women disciples were unusually privileged to have a central role in Jesus' ministry, and we were not relegated to do only the housekeeping either. I remember well when Jesus, my beloved Rabboni, praised Mary of Bethany for her attentive listening to his teaching. Jesus took women's talents seriously, and his friendships and conversations with women shocked many observers— even producing resistance from some of his male disciples.

When modern folk read and study the Scriptures today they can be enlightened by so much new biblical scholarship; they can hear and understand the word of God in enriched ways. Our sacred word is like the mustard seed that grows and grows into a huge tree; our retreatants should always read and meditate upon the word because the Good News is like yeast which leavens our individual spiritual journeys, as well as changing the course of history.

**Augustine:** Yes, I have been much concerned trying to work out a Christian understanding of human history. Many pagan Romans of my day blamed Christians for the fall of the Roman empire and I had to answer their charges. I have always tried to understand God's care and plan for his created world. But, as in every scholarly work that I attempted, I began to see that as we love God more, we will understand more—and there will always be more to understand. The mystery of God, the Author of Life, is infinite and beyond all human imagination.

**Mary:** This is why we Christians need the support of our fellow Church members as we journey together into the mystery of God's life for us. We need to keep each other company on the pilgrimage, to offer one another encouragement and correct each other's biases. With, in and through Christ and the Church we keep our balance and can persevere on a steadfast course. Within the Church and the Catholic center we can steer clear of either simpleminded, superficial approaches to religion or of over-rationalized elitist interpretations of the gospel.

I would advise our retreatants not only to read and study on their own but to join fully in the life and worship of the Church. The community of saints and our immensely complex and rich Christian heritage nourish us. Moreover, the wonderful promise has been made that we in the Church can continue Christ's work in the world through the ages. All of us take part in the transformation of God's good creation and help the Kingdom come. I like Saint Paul's image of the whole creation groaning in childbirth waiting on our transformation and salvation.

Whatever our life situation, if we seek God, if we ask, the Spirit will help renew our hearts and minds and deeds.

Christians called to live in Christian marriage have an especially important role in transforming the world. A married couple and the family they create has been called the Church in miniature; each household is a primary cell of the larger Church body. If in our retreat we can help Christians understand love, sex and marriage—and to live in love more abundantly, they will form the Church of today and tomorrow.

Augustine prays:

O Lord our God, let the shelter of your wings give us hope. Protect us and uphold us. You will be the Support that upholds us from childhood till the hair on our heads is grey. When you are our strength we are strong, but when our strength is our own we are weak. In you our good abides for ever, and when we turn away from it we turn to evil. Let us come home at last to you, O Lord, for fear that we be lost. For in you our good abides and it has no blemish, since it is yourself. Nor do we fear that there is no home to which we can return. We fell from it; but our home is your eternity and it does not fall because we are away.[4]

## Notes

[1] *Confessions*, Book IV, 15, p. 86.

[2] *The Good of Marriage*, Chapter 16, p. 32.

[3] *Confessions*, Book XII, 25, p. 301.

[4] Ibid., Book IV, p. 16.

# Deepening Your Acquaintance

## With Mary of Magdala

### Books

Fiorenza, Elisabeth Schussler. *In Memory of Her: A Feminist Theological Reconstruction of Christian Origins*. New York: Crossroad, 1988.

Haskins, Susan. *Mary Magdalen: Myth and Metaphor*. New York: Harcourt Brace & Company, 1993.

Ricci, Carla. *Mary Magdalene and Many Others: Women who followed Jesus*, trans. Paul Burns. Minneapolis, Minn.: Augsburg Fortress, 1994.

Thompson, Mary R., S.S.M.N. *Mary of Magdala: Apostle and Leader*. New York: Paulist Press, 1995.

### Video

*Mary Magdalene: An Intimate Portrait*. Paulist Press.


## With Augustine

### Books

Saint Augustine. *City of God*, trans. Henry Bettenson. New York: Penguin Classics, 1984.

_____. *Confessions*, trans. R.S. Pine-Coffin. New York: Penguin Classics, 1961.

Bourke, Vernon J. *The Essential Augustine: Selected and with Commentary by Vernon J. Bourke.* Indianapolis: Hackett Publishing Company, 1974.

Brown, Peter. *Augustine of Hippo: A Biography.* Berkeley, Calif.: University of California Press, 1967.

_____. *The Body and Society: Men, Women, and Sexual Renunciation in Early Christianity.* New York: Columbia University Press, 1988.

*The Fathers of the Church* Series devoted to St. Augustine, Editorial Director, Ludwig Schopp, Volumes 5, 16, 27. New York: CIMA Publishing Co., Inc., 1948.